Programming in
QuickBASIC

SHELLY
CASHMAN
SERIES

Programming in QuickBASIC

JAMES S. QUASNEY

boyd & fraser

bf

boyd & fraser publishing company

© 1992 by boyd & fraser publishing company
A Division of South-Western Publishing Company
Boston, MA 02116

Developed by Susan Solomon Communications
Manufactured in the United States of America

ISBN 0-87835-777-7

3 4 5 6 W 5 4 3

CONTENTS IN BRIEF

CONTENTS

Programming in QuickBASIC

APPENDIX   QuickBASIC DEBUGGING TECHNIQUES   QB 115

PREFACE

Programming in QuickBASIC is designed for a first course on Microsoft QuickBASIC programming. It introduces fundamental programming concepts, presents the essentials of the Microsoft QuickBASIC language, and acquaints students with structured and top-down programming techniques. This book assumes neither previous experience with computers nor mathematics beyond the high school freshman level. It incorporates salient material from, and is based upon the methodology and pedagogy of, earlier works by Gary B. Shelly and Thomas J. Cashman.

ORGANIZATION OF THE TEXTBOOK

The content of this textbook is organized into six projects. In each project a problem is presented and then, step by step, it is thoroughly solved with a QuickBASIC program.

Project 1 — An Introduction to Programming in QuickBASIC

This first project introduces students to the program development cycle, the basic characteristics of a QuickBASIC program, and the QuickBASIC operating environment.

Project 2 — Basic Arithmetic Operations and Accumulating Totals

Project 2 presents computations, summary totals, report editing, and printing a report.

Project 3 — Decisions

In this project students learn about decision making. Topics include the IF statement, implementing If-Then-Else structures, logical operators, and the SELECT CASE statement.

Project 4 — Interactive Programming, For Loops, and an Introduction to the Top-Down Approach

Unlike the first three projects, which use the READ and DATA statements to integrate data into a program, Project 4 shows students how to use the INPUT statement to accomplish this task. Also included is coverage of how to use For loops to implement counter-controlled loops, and how to design top-down programs.

Project 5 — Sequential File Processing

This project introduces students to creating and processing a sequential data file.

Project 6 — Arrays and Functions

In this final project students learn how to write programs that can look up information in tables; they are then acquainted with the most often used QuickBASIC *built-in* functions.

Appendix — QuickBASIC Debugging Techniques

This appendix introduces students to the debugging features that are built into Microsoft QuickBASIC, specifically the immediate window, stepping one statement at a time, breakpoints, tracing, recording, and watchpoints.

Reference Card

Included at the back of this book is a reference card that lists all of the statements, functions, and features of Microsoft QuickBASIC.

EXERCISES AND ASSIGNMENTS

 ach project includes one or more sets of Try It Yourself Exercises and Student Programming Assignments.

Try It Yourself Exercises

These are paper-and-pencil exercises to help students master the concepts presented. Over 75 such exercises are included; some are complete programs. Also instructors can use these exercises as a diagnostic tool.

Student Programming Assignments

These field-tested assignments are included at the end of each project. Each assignment includes instructions, sample input data, and sample output results.

INSTRUCTOR'S MATERIALS

*T*he Instructor's Materials supplement includes the following:

- Lesson Plans with lecture outlines and notes
- Answers/solutions to all Try It Yourself Exercises and Student Assignments
- Test questions with answer key
- Transparency Masters for every figure
- Instructor's Diskette containing the files used in *Introduction to DOS*, and the program solutions to all Student Assignments. This is included in both 3 1/2" and 5 1/4" formats.

ACKNOWLEDGMENTS

*O*ur thanks to the many talented individuals who contributed to the quality of this book. Special thanks to John Maniotes, Diane Larson, Pat Stephan, Anne Craig, Ginny Harvey, Jeanne Huntington, Ken Russo, Becky Herrington, Susan Solomon, and Tom Walker.

Programming in QuickBASIC

QuickBASIC PROJECTS

PROJECT 1

An Introduction to Programming in QuickBASIC

*I*n Project 1 we provide an introduction to the principles of program design and computer programming using the QuickBASIC programming language. QuickBASIC was developed for the personal computer (PC) by Microsoft Corporation, one of the largest microcomputer software companies in the world. Today, QuickBASIC is one of the most widely used programming languages on PCs.

Our approach in illustrating QuickBASIC is to present a series of applications that can be processed using a PC. We carefully explain the input data, the output to be produced, and the processing. Through the use of a flowchart, we illustrate the program design and logic. The flowchart is followed by an explanation of the QuickBASIC statements required to implement the logic. We then present the complete QuickBASIC program. The program solution, when entered into the PC and executed, will produce the output from the specified input.

THE PROGRAMMING PROCESS

*C*omputer programs can vary significantly in size and complexity. A simple program may contain only a few statements. A complex program can contain hundreds and even thousands of statements. Regardless of the size of the program, it is extremely important that the task of computer programming be approached in a professional manner, as computer programming is one of the most precise of all activities.

Learning computer programming should not be approached as a trial-and-error-type of activity. By carefully reviewing the sample problems, the program design, and the QuickBASIC code we present within these projects, you should be able to write well-designed programs that produce correct output when executed on a PC.

Computer programming is not *naturally* an error-prone activity. Errors enter into the design and coding of the computer program only through carelessness or lack of understanding of the programming process. With careful study and attention to detail, you can avoid errors. Just as it is the job of the accountant, the mathematician, the engineer, and the scientist to produce correct results, so too it is the job of the computer programmer to produce a program that is reliable, easy to read, and produces accurate results.

The actual programming process involves the activities described in Figure 1-1. When you use this careful approach to program design and coding, you can develop programs that are easy to read, efficient, reliable, and execute properly.

STEP	DESCRIPTION
1	Define the problem to be solved precisely in terms of input, processing, and output.
2	Design a detailed logic plan using flowcharts or some other logic tool.
3	Desk check the logic plan as if you are the computer.
4	Code the program.
5	Desk check the code as if you are the computer.
6	Enter the program into the computer.
7	Test the program until it is error free.
8	Run the program using the input data to generate the output results.

FIGURE 1-1 The program development cycle

SAMPLE PROGRAM 1 — PATIENT LISTING

 n this first sample program we generate a patient listing on the screen. The input data consists of the series of patient records shown in Figure 1-2. Each record contains a patient name, a doctor name, and a room number.

PATIENT NAME	DOCTOR NAME	ROOM NUMBER
Tim Krel	Nance	112
Mary Lepo	Gold	102
Tom Pep	King	245
Joe Ruiz	Ward	213
EOF	End	0

FIGURE 1-2   The patient records

The data taken as a group is called a **file**. The data about a single individual is called a **record**. Each unit of data within the record is called a **field**, or **data item**. Thus, the input data consists of a file of patient records. Each record contains a patient name field, a doctor name field, and a room number field.

In the list of records in Figure 1-2, the last record contains the patient name EOF, the doctor name End, and the room number 0. This record is called a trailer record, or sentinel record. A **trailer record** is added to the end of the file to indicate when all the valid records have been processed.

The output for this sample program is a listing on the PC screen of each record in the patient file. The output listing is shown in Figure 1-3.

```
        Patient Listing

Room           Patient        Doctor

  112          Tim Krel       Nance
  102          Mary Lepo      Gold
  245          Tom Pep        King
  213          Joe Ruiz       Ward

End of Patient List
```

FIGURE 1-3   The required output for Sample Program 1

The patient list includes the room number, the patient name, and the doctor name for each record. Notice that the sequence of the fields displayed on the screen is different from the sequence of the fields in the input record. Column headings identify each field. After all records have been processed, the message End of Patient List displays.

Program Flowchart

The flowchart, QuickBASIC program, and output for Sample Program 1 are shown in Figure 1-4. The flowchart illustrates a simple looping structure. After the headings are displayed, a record is read. This read statement, prior to the loop, is called a **primary read**, or **lead read**.

A. PROGRAM FLOWCHART

B. PROGRAM LISTING

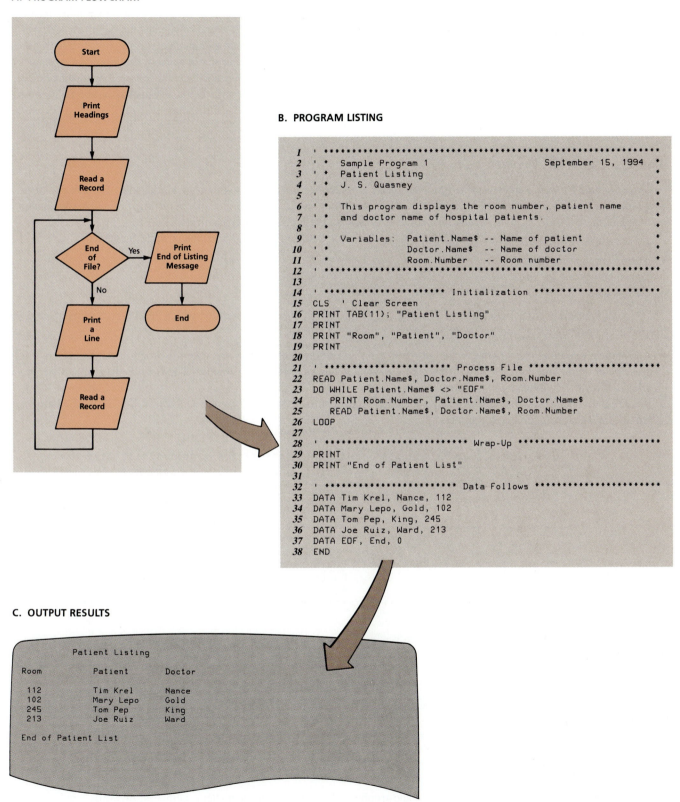

C. OUTPUT RESULTS

FIGURE 1-4   The program flowchart (A), program listing (B), and output results (C) for Sample Program 1

Following the lead read in the program flowchart in Figure 1-4, a test is performed to determine if the record just read was the trailer record containing the patient name EOF. If so, there are no more records to process. If not, then more records remain to be processed. This decision determines if the loop should be entered. If the end-of-file has not been reached, the loop is entered. Within the loop the previously read record is displayed on the screen and another record is read. Control then returns to the decision symbol at the top of the loop. As long as the trailer record has not been read, the looping continues.

When the trailer record is read, the looping process stops and an end-of-job message displays followed by termination of the program. This basic logic is appropriate for all applications which involve reading records and displaying the fields from the record read on an output device.

The QuickBASIC Program

Programs should be well documented, easy to read, easy to understand, and easy to modify and maintain. For these reasons, programming standards have been developed to guide the beginning programmer in the task of writing programs. We illustrate and explain these standards in all sample programs we present in these programming projects.

A program written using QuickBASIC consists of a series of statements which serve one of three functions:

1. Document the program
2. Cause processing to occur
3. Define data

A quality program is well documented. This means the program contains information which helps a reader understand the program. Documentation within the program should include the following:

- A prologue, including the program name, program title, an author identification, the date the program was written, a brief description of the program, and a description of the variable names used in the program. The first 12 lines of Sample Program 1 (Figure 1-5) contain the prologue.
- Remark lines should come before any major module in a program. In Sample Program 1, lines 14, 21, 28, and 32 are remark lines that precede major modules.

FIGURE 1-5
The prologue for Sample Program 1

```
 1  ' ***************************************************************
 2  ' *  Sample Program 1                    September 15, 1994  *
 3  ' *  Patient Listing                                         *
 4  ' *  J. S. Quasney                                           *
 5  ' *                                                          *
 6  ' *  This program displays the room number, patient name,    *
 7  ' *  and doctor name of hospital patients.                   *
 8  ' *                                                          *
 9  ' *  Variables:  Patient.Name$ -- Name of patient            *
10  ' *              Doctor.Name$  -- Name of doctor             *
11  ' *              Room.Number   -- Room number                *
12  ' ***************************************************************
```

Documentation within a QuickBASIC program is accomplished through the use of the REM statement. The general form of the REM statement is shown in Figure 1-6.

FIGURE 1-6
The general form of the REM statement

```
REM comment

   or

' comment
```

The remark statement begins with REM or an apostrophe (') followed by any characters, numbers, or words required to document the program. Notice that in these programming projects, we use the apostrophe (') rather than the keyword REM to initiate a remark line. Asterisks (*) are used in the remark lines to highlight the documentation.

Blank lines, such as lines 13, 20, 27, and 31 of Sample Program 1 (Figure 1-4), are used to end any major module. For example, the Initialization module (Figure 1-7) begins with a remark line and ends with a blank line. The proper use of remark lines, blank lines, and indentations can substantially improve the readability of a program. We suggest that you follow the format illustrated in Sample Program 1 when coding all QuickBASIC programs.

The apostrophe (') can also be used to include in-line remarks as shown following the CLS statement in line 15 of Figure 1-7. All characters that follows the apostrophe in an in-line remark are considered to be part of the documentation.

Remember that remark lines and blank lines can be added before or after any line in a program. In addition, they are strictly for human comprehension and have no effect on the outcome of the program.

```
14  ' ******************** Initialization ********************
15  CLS  ' Clear Screen
16  PRINT TAB(11); "Patient Listing"
17  PRINT
18  PRINT "Room", "Patient", "Doctor"
19  PRINT
20
```

FIGURE 1-7
The Initialization module of Sample Program 1

THE DATA STATEMENT

Sample Program 1 employs DATA statements to define the data. The DATA statements for Sample Program 1 are shown in Figure 1-8.

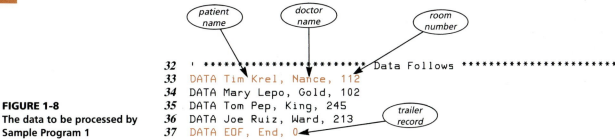

```
32  ' ******************** Data Follows ********************
33  DATA Tim Krel, Nance, 112
34  DATA Mary Lepo, Gold, 102
35  DATA Tom Pep, King, 245
36  DATA Joe Ruiz, Ward, 213
37  DATA EOF, End, 0
```

FIGURE 1-8
The data to be processed by Sample Program 1

In Figure 1-8, line 33 defines the first patient record. Line 34 defines the second patient record, and so on. DATA statements begin with the keyword DATA followed by a space and the data. The DATA statement in line 33 contains the patient name (Tim Krel), the doctor name (Nance), and the room number (112). As shown in Figure 1-8, each of the data items must be separated by a comma.

The last DATA statement is the trailer record, when a trailer record is used in this manner, you must include an entry for each field. In line 37, the phrase EOF is included for the patient name, the word End is included in place of the doctor name, and the numeric value 0 is included for the room number. These values, of course, will not be included in the listing generated by the program.

The general form of the DATA statement is shown in Figure 1-9.

FIGURE 1-9
The general form of the DATA statement

> DATA data item, data item, ..., data item
>
> where each data item is a numeric or string value

THE CLS, PRINT, AND END STATEMENTS

U p to this point, we have talked about REM and DATA statements. Both of these statements are classified as nonexecutable. Neither type of statement has anything to do with the logic shown in the flowchart in Figure 1-4. For example, the DATA statements can be moved from the bottom of the program to the top of the program with no effect on the logic of the program.

In this section we discuss the CLS, PRINT, and END statements.

The CLS Statement

The first executable statement in Sample Program 1 is the CLS statement in line 15 (Figure 1-10). The function of this statement is to clear the output screen and move the cursor to the upper left corner. The **output screen** is the one that shows the results due to the execution of a program.

```
14  ' ******************** Initialization ********************
15  CLS  ' Clear Screen
16  PRINT TAB(11); "Patient Listing"
17  PRINT
18  PRINT "Room", "Patient", "Doctor"
19  PRINT
20
```

FIGURE 1-10
The Initialization module of Sample Program 1

The PRINT Statement

The PRINT statement is used to write information on the output screen. It is commonly used to display headings and the values of variables and control spacing in a report. As shown in Figure 1-11, the PRINT statement consists of the keyword PRINT. It may also have an optional list of print items separated by commas and semicolons.

FIGURE 1-11
The general form of the PRINT statement

> PRINT list
>
> where **list** is the items to display separated by semicolons or commas

The list in a PRINT statement includes print items. The **print items** can be any of the following:

- Variables, such as Doctor.Name$, Patient.Name$, and Room.Number
- Constants, such as numeric and string values—string values must be enclosed in quotation marks (")
- Function references, such as the TAB function—the TAB function allows you to move the cursor to the right to a specified column position

Lines 16 through 19 of Sample Program 1 (Figure 1-10) display the report title and column headings. Line 16 displays the report title on line 1. The first print item in line 16 is the TAB function. It causes the cursor to move to column 11. The semicolon following the TAB function instructs the PC to display the next print item (Patient Listing) at the current cursor location (column 11). Hence, the report title Patient Listing displays beginning in column 11 on line 1. After line 16 is executed, the cursor moves down one line on the output screen to line 2.

The PRINT statement in line 17 contains no print items. A PRINT statement with no print items causes the PC to skip a line. Thus, line 2 on the output screen is left blank.

Line 18 displays the three column headings. Each column heading is surrounded by the required quotation marks. Notice that the column headings also are separated by commas. When the print items are separated by commas, the fields are displayed in predefined columns called print zones. There are five print zones per line. Each **print zone** has 14 positions for a total of 70 positions per line as shown in Figure 1-12.

FIGURE 1-12
There are five print zones of 14 positions each for a total of 70 positions

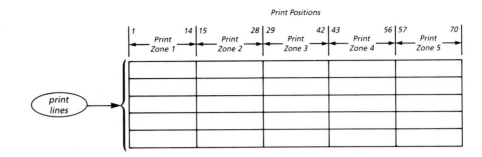

When line 18 in Sample Program 1 executes, Room displays beginning in column 1, Patient displays beginning in column 15, and Doctor displays beginning in column 29. Like line 17, line 19 causes the PC to skip a line on the output screen.

The END Statement

The last line in Sample Program 1 is the END statement. When executed, the END statement instructs the PC to stop executing the program. Although the END statement is not required, it is recommended that you always include one.

VARIABLES

*I*n programming, a **variable** is a location in main memory whose value can change as the program executes. There are two major categories of variables—numeric and string. A **numeric variable** can only be assigned a numeric value. A **string variable** may be assigned a string of characters such as a word, name, phrase, or sentence.

A **variable name** is used to define and reference a variable in main memory. Variable names must conform to certain rules. In QuickBASIC, a variable name begins with a letter and may be followed by up to 39 letters, digits, and decimal points. You may not use a QuickBASIC keyword, such as CLS or PRINT, as a variable name. For a complete list of the Quick-BASIC keywords, refer to the last page of the reference card at the back of this book.

String variable names always end with a dollar sign ($). Numeric variable names never end with a dollar sign. For example, in Sample Program 1, Room.Number is a numeric variable and Patient.Name$ and Doctor.Name$ are string variables.

With respect to the variable names used in Sample Program 1, notice how we use the decimal point (.) to better describe what the variables will hold during the execution of the program.

THE READ STATEMENT

*T*o assign the data in the DATA statements to variables, we use the READ statement. As shown in Figure 1-13, the READ statement consists of the keyword READ followed by one or more variable names separated from each other by commas. The variable names must be specified in the READ statement in the order in which the data is recorded in the DATA statements.

FIGURE 1-13
The general form of the READ statement

READ variable$_1$, variable$_2$, ..., variable$_n$

where each variable is a numeric variable or string variable

When line 22 (Figure 1-14) is executed, the first data item is assigned to the first variable in the READ statement. Thus, Tim Krel is assigned to Patient.Name$. The second data item (Nance) is assigned to Doctor.Name$ and the third data item (112) is assigned to Room.Number.

Refer to Sample Program 1 in Figure 1-4 and notice that the READ statement in line 22 has the same number of variables as the DATA statements have data items. In other words, each time a READ statement is executed, one DATA statement is used. Although we recommend this style, it is not required. For example, the following shows that it is valid to write the READ statement in line 22 as three READ statements:

```
READ Patient.Name$
READ Doctor.Name$
READ Room.Number
DATA Tim Krel, Nance, 112
```

We could have also placed one data item per DATA statement as follows:

```
READ Patient.Name$, Doctor.Name$, Room.Number
DATA Tim Krel
DATA Nance
DATA 112
```

THE DO WHILE AND LOOP STATEMENTS

Following the first READ statement in line 22, lines 23 through 26 establish a **Do loop** (Figure 1-14). The DO WHILE statement in line 23 and the LOOP statement in line 26 cause the range of statements between them to be executed repeatedly as long as Patient.Name$ does not equal the string value EOF. The expression Patient.Name$ <> "EOF" following DO WHILE in line 23 is called a **condition**. A condition can be true or false. In the case of the DO WHILE, the statements within the loop are executed while the condition is true.

```
21  ' ********************** Process File **********************
22  READ Patient.Name$, Doctor.Name$, Room.Number
23  DO WHILE Patient.Name$ <> "EOF"
24     PRINT Room.Number, Patient.Name$, Doctor.Name$
25     READ Patient.Name$, Doctor.Name$, Room.Number
26  LOOP
27
28  ' ********************** Wrap-Up **********************
29  PRINT
30  PRINT "End of Patient List"
31
```

FIGURE 1-14
The Process File and Wrap-Up modules of Sample Program 1

When Patient.Name$ does equal EOF, the condition in line 23 is false. Therefore, the PC skips the statements within the loop and continues execution at the first executable statement following the corresponding LOOP statement. The first executable statement following the LOOP statement is the PRINT statement in line 29.

One execution of a Do loop is called a **pass**. The statements within the loop, lines 24 and 25, are indented by three spaces for the purpose of readability. Collectively, lines 24 and 25 are called the **range** of statements in the Do loop.

Following execution of the lead read in line 22, Patient.Name$ is equal to Tim Krel. Hence, control passes into the Do loop and the first patient record is displayed due to the PRINT statement in line 24. Next, the READ statement in line 25 assigns the variables Patient.Name$, Doctor.Name$, and Room.Number the data items found in the second DATA statement. The LOOP statement in line 26 automatically returns control to the DO WHILE statement in line 23. This process continues while Patient.Name$ does not equal EOF.

The general forms of the DO WHILE and LOOP statements are shown in Figure 1-15.

FIGURE 1-15
The general forms of the DO
WHILE and LOOP statements

```
DO WHILE condition

    [range of statements]

LOOP
```

Testing for the End-of-File

Lines 33 through 36 in Sample Program 1 (Figure 1-4) contain data for only four patients. The fifth patient in line 37 is the **trailer record**. It represents the end-of-file and is used to determine when all the valid data has been processed. To incorporate an end-of-file test, a variable must be selected and a trailer record added to the data. We selected the patient name as the test for end-of-file and the data value EOF. Since it guards against reading past end-of-file, the trailer record is also called the **sentinel record**. The value EOF is called the **sentinel value**. The value EOF is clearly distinguishable from all the rest of the data assigned to Patient.Name$. This sentinel value is the same as the string constant found in the condition in line 23.

After the READ statement in line 25 assigns Patient.Name$ the value EOF, the LOOP statement returns control to the DO WHILE statement. Since Patient.Name$ is equal to the value EOF, the DO WHILE statement causes the PC to pass control to line 29 which follows the corresponding LOOP statement. Line 29 skips a line and line 30 displays an end-of-job message. Lines 29 and 30 are referred to as an **end-of-file routine**.

Three other worthy points to consider about establishing a test for end-of-file in a Do loop are:

1. It is important that the trailer record contain enough values for all the variables in the READ statement. In Sample Program 1, if we only added the sentinel value EOF to line 37, there would not be enough data to fulfill the requirements of the three variables in the READ statement. We arbitrarily assigned End and 0 to the second and third variables in the READ statement.
2. The Do loop requires the use of two READ statements. The first READ statement (line 22) reads the first patient record before the PC enters the Do loop. The second READ statement, found at the bottom of the Do loop (line 25), causes the PC to read the next data record. This READ statement reads the remaining data records, one at a time, until there are no more data records left. If the first record contains the patient name EOF, the DO WHILE statement will immediately transfer control to the statement below the corresponding LOOP statement.
3. Sample Program 1 can process any number of patients by placing each in a DATA statement prior to the trailer record.

Conditions

The DO WHILE statement in line 23 (Figure 1-14) contains the condition

```
Patient.Name$ <> "EOF"
```

The condition is made up of two expressions and a **relational operator**. The condition specifies a relationship between expressions that is either true or false. If the condition is true, execution continues with the line following the DO WHILE statement. If the condition is false, then control is transferred to the line following the corresponding LOOP statement.

The PC makes a comparison between the two operators based on the relational operator. Figure 1-16 lists the six valid relational operators.

FIGURE 1-16
Relational operators used in
conditions

RELATION	MATH SYMBOL	QuickBASIC SYMBOL	EXAMPLE
Equal To	=	=	Educ$ = "12"
Less Than	<	<	Total < 25
Greater Than	>	>	Disc > .15
Less Than Or Equal To	≤	<= or =<	Deduc <= 10
Greater Than Or Equal To	≥	>= or =>	Code$ >= "A"
Not Equal To	≠	<> or ><	State$ <> "TX"

There are several important points to watch for in the application of conditions. For example, it is invalid to compare a numeric variable to a string value as in the following:

```
DO WHILE Cents > "10"
```

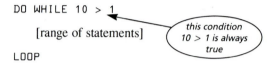

this condition Cents > "10" is invalid

Furthermore, the condition should ensure termination of the loop. For example, look at the following logical error:

```
DO WHILE 10 > 1
    [range of statements]
LOOP
```

this condition 10 > 1 is always true

If such an error is not detected, a never-ending loop develops. There is no way to stop the endless program execution except by manual intervention, such as pressing **Ctrl + Break** on your PC keyboard. (The plus sign between two keys means hold down the first key and press the second key, and then release both keys.)

The complete QuickBASIC program and the output results are again illustrated in Figures 1-17 and 1-18.

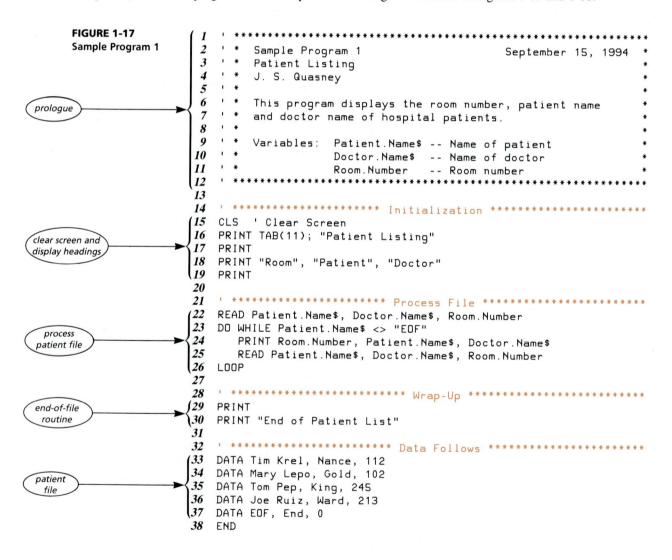

FIGURE 1-17
Sample Program 1

prologue

clear screen and display headings

process patient file

end-of-file routine

patient file

```
1  ' ************************************************************
2  ' *  Sample Program 1                    September 15, 1994  *
3  ' *  Patient Listing                                         *
4  ' *  J. S. Quasney                                           *
5  ' *                                                          *
6  ' *  This program displays the room number, patient name     *
7  ' *  and doctor name of hospital patients.                   *
8  ' *                                                          *
9  ' *  Variables:  Patient.Name$ -- Name of patient            *
10 ' *              Doctor.Name$ -- Name of doctor              *
11 ' *              Room.Number  -- Room number                 *
12 ' ************************************************************
13
14 ' ********************* Initialization *********************
15 CLS  ' Clear Screen
16 PRINT TAB(11); "Patient Listing"
17 PRINT
18 PRINT "Room", "Patient", "Doctor"
19 PRINT
20
21 ' ********************* Process File *********************
22 READ Patient.Name$, Doctor.Name$, Room.Number
23 DO WHILE Patient.Name$ <> "EOF"
24    PRINT Room.Number, Patient.Name$, Doctor.Name$
25    READ Patient.Name$, Doctor.Name$, Room.Number
26 LOOP
27
28 ' ********************* Wrap-Up *********************
29 PRINT
30 PRINT "End of Patient List"
31
32 ' ********************* Data Follows *********************
33 DATA Tim Krel, Nance, 112
34 DATA Mary Lepo, Gold, 102
35 DATA Tom Pep, King, 245
36 DATA Joe Ruiz, Ward, 213
37 DATA EOF, End, 0
38 END
```

FIGURE 1-18
The output results due to the execution of Sample Program 1

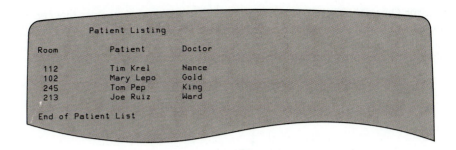

```
          Patient Listing

Room          Patient        Doctor

  112         Tim Krel       Nance
  102         Mary Lepo      Gold
  245         Tom Pep        King
  213         Joe Ruiz       Ward

End of Patient List
```

TRY IT YOURSELF EXERCISES

1. Which of the following are valid numeric variables in QuickBASIC?
   a. X$
   b. Account
   c. 8T
   d. Inventory.No

2. Write a CLS statement and a series of PRINT statements that display the value LINE 1 beginning in column 1 of line 1, LINE 3 in column 1 of line 3, and LINE 5 in column 1 of line 5.

3. Write a PRINT statement that displays the string values Name, Account, Balance, Date in print zones 1 through 4 of the current line.

4. Use the TAB function in a PRINT statement to display the string value The answer is beginning in column 42 of the current line.

5. Given the following DATA statement:

   DATA 16723, 12, 56

   Use the variables Inventory.Number, On.Order, and On.Hand to write a READ statement that assigns Inventory.Number the value 16723, On.Order the value 12, and On.Hand the value 56.

6. State the purpose of the LOOP statement.

7. List and describe the six relational operators.

8. Which of the following are invalid DO WHILE statements? Why?
   a. DO WHILE X = 10
   b. DOWHILE Acct$ <> "End"
   c. DO WHILE 5 < Tax
   d. DO WHILE On.Hand LT 25
   e. DO WHILE Volts Equals 37

9. Determine whether the conditions below are true or false, given the following: Hours = 6, Tonnage = 12.5, and Bonus = 1.75
   a. Hours >= 10
   b. Tonnage >= 12
   c. Bonus <> 2
   d. Hours <> 6
   e. Tonnage < 12.5
   f. Bonus = 1.75

10. Write the QuickBASIC code for the Process File and Wrap-Up modules that correspond to the following program flow-chart. Use the variable names specified in the Read and Print symbols. Do not include any DATA statements. Start each module with a remark line and end each module with a blank line. For the end-of-file test, assume the trailer record includes the following data items: EOF, 0, 0.

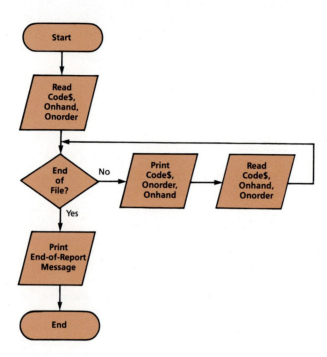

THE QB OPERATING ENVIRONMENT

To enter a program such as Sample Program 1 into the PC and execute it, you must familiarize yourself with the QB operating environment.

Starting a Session

Boot the PC using the steps outlined by your instructor, or those found in the PC's Operations manual. Once the PC is operational, do the following:

1. Place the QuickBASIC program disk in the default drive and your data disk in the other drive.
2. At the DOS prompt, enter QBI if you are using the textbook version of QuickBASIC or QB if you are using the commercial version of QuickBASIC.

Several seconds will elapse while the QuickBASIC program is loaded from the disk into main memory. The red light on the disk drive turns on during this loading process. After the QuickBASIC program is loaded into main storage, it is automatically executed.

The first screen displayed by QuickBASIC includes a Welcome message in the middle of the screen. In the Welcome message, QuickBASIC directs you to press the **Esc key** to begin entering a program or press the **Enter key** to obtain help from the QB Advisor. The **QB Advisor** is an on-line help system that answers your questions about QuickBASIC as fast as you can click the mouse or press the **F1 key**. The QB Advisor is discussed in more detail later in this section.

The QB Screen

There are four parts to the QB screen—the view window, menu bar, immediate window, and the status line. These are shown in Figure 1-19.

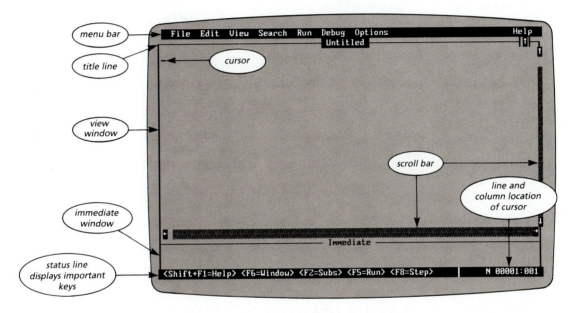

FIGURE 1-19   The QB (QuickBASIC) screen

View Window   The **view window** is the largest part of the screen and the one that contains the cursor (Figure 1-19). In the view window you can enter, modify, and display programs. When the QuickBASIC program first executes, the view window is active. That is, if you start typing characters, they will appear on the first line of the view window. At the top of the view window is the title line. The **title line** displays the name of the current program. The program title is highlighted when the view window is active. The program is called "Untitled" until it is given a name. Program names will be discussed shortly.

Along the bottom and the right side of the view window are the **scroll bars**. If you have a mouse, you can move the pointer along the scroll bars and move the window in any direction to see code that does not appear in the view window.

Menu Bar   The **menu bar**, the line at the very top of the QB screen (Figure 1-19), displays a list of menu names. Each menu name has a corresponding menu of commands. These commands are useful when entering and modifying programs.

To activate the menu bar, press the **Alt key**. Next, type the first letter of the name of the menu you want to open. You can also select a menu by using the **Right Arrow key** or the **Left Arrow key** to highlight the menu name. With the menu name highlighted, press the **Enter key**. QuickBASIC immediately displays a *pull-down menu* that lists a series of commands. Figure 1-20 shows the **File menu**, which is superimposed over the display of Sample Program 1. To deactivate the menu bar or any menu and activate the view window, press the **Esc key**.

FIGURE 1-20
The File menu

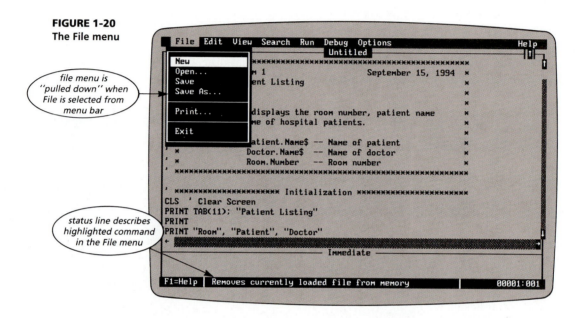

If your PC has a mouse, move the mouse pointer to the desired menu name and click the mouse button. The **mouse pointer** is a character-size, rectangular box on the screen. The **mouse button** is the left button on the mouse. To deactivate the menu bar and reactivate the view window, move the mouse pointer to any part of the view window and click the mouse button.

Immediate Window   The narrow window below the view window is called the **immediate window**. The immediate window is used to execute statements as soon as they are entered. Statements entered in the immediate window are not part of the current program.

At any time, you can activate the immediate window by pressing the function key **F6**. This moves the cursor from the view window to the immediate window. QuickBASIC highlights the word Immediate. The function key **F6** is like a **toggle switch**. Press it once, and the cursor moves from the view window to the immediate window. Press it again, and the cursor moves back to the view window. You may use the immediate window as a calculator and debugging tool. For more information on the use of the immediate window, refer to the section titled Debugging Techniques in the Appendix.

If you have a mouse, move the pointer to the inactive window and click the mouse button.

Status Line   The line at the very bottom of the QB screen (Figure 1-19) is the **status line**. This line contains a list of the most often used function keys and the line and column location of the cursor on the screen. Keyboard indicators, such as C for Caps Lock and N for Num Lock, display immediately to the left of the cursor line and column location counter when these keys are engaged.

If the menu bar is active and one of the menus is selected, then the status line displays the function of the highlighted command in the menu (Figure 1-20).

Dialog Boxes

QuickBASIC uses **dialog boxes** to display messages and request information from you. For example, if you use a keyword for a variable name, such as PRINT LET instead of PRINT BET, QuickBASIC displays a dialog box when you move the cursor off the line containing the invalid variable name LET. You move the cursor off the line by pressing the **Enter key** or the **Up Arrow key** or **Down Arrow key**.

The dialog box shown in Figure 1-21 displays if you attempt to end the QuickBASIC session and return control to DOS without saving the latest changes made to the current program. Dialog boxes list acceptable user responses in buttons and text boxes. **Buttons** are labeled to indicate what they represent. **Text boxes** are used to enter information such as a file name.

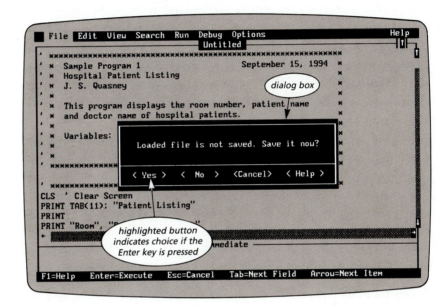

FIGURE 1-21
QuickBASIC displays a dialog box in the middle of the view window when it requires a response from the user before it can continue

In response to the message in the dialog box in Figure 1-21, you can use the **Tab key** or mouse pointer to select one of four buttons—Yes, No, Cancel, or Help. When you press the **Enter key**, the highlighted button, the one with the cursor, is selected. If your PC has a mouse, move the mouse pointer to the desired button or text box and click the mouse button.

Cursor Movement Keys

Several keys on the keyboard are used to move the cursor on the screen. These keys are called the **cursor movement keys**. The arrow keys are used to move the cursor in the windows, menu bar, or menu, one position at a time. Other keys such as the **Home key** and **End key** are used to move the cursor more than one position at a time. The cursor movement keys are summarized on the last page of the reference card at the back of this book.

Function Keys

IBM-type keyboards include a set of ten or twelve **function keys**, which are located to the far left side of the keyboard or along the top of the typewriter keys. The function keys are labeled **F1** through **F10** or **F12**. Pressing these keys instructs QuickBASIC to carry out various tasks. For example, if you press function key **F1** with the cursor in a keyword, QuickBASIC displays a help screen. If you press **Shift + F5**, QuickBASIC executes the current program in the view window. For a complete list of the function keys, refer to the last page of the reference card at the back of this book.

Terminating a QuickBASIC Session

To terminate your QuickBASIC session, press the **Alt key** to activate the menu bar. With the cursor on the word **File**, type the letter **F** or press the **Enter key** to display the **File menu** (Figure 1-20). Next, type the letter **X** for **Exit** or use the arrow keys to move the cursor to the word Exit and press the **Enter key**. Thus, the sequence of keystrokes **Alt**, **F**, **X** instructs the PC to return control to DOS. To quit QuickBASIC using a mouse, click on **File** in the menu bar and click on **Exit** in the **File menu**. The term *click on* means move the mouse pointer to the specified word and click the mouse button.

If you did not save the latest version of the current program, then the dialog box shown earlier in Figure 1-21 appears. QuickBASIC requests that you select one of the buttons before continuing. An alternative to selecting a button is to press the **Esc key**, which cancels the command and returns control to the view window.

When the DOS prompt appears, remove your diskettes from the disk drives. Turn the PC's power switch to Off. Turn the monitor power switch to Off. Finally, if you are using a printer, turn the power switch to Off.

Editing QuickBASIC Programs

QuickBASIC programs are entered one line at a time into the view window. The **Enter key** signals QuickBASIC that a line is complete. During the process of entering a program, you will quickly learn that it is easy to make keyboard errors and grammatical errors because of your inexperience with the QuickBASIC language and your unfamiliarity with the keyboard. Logical errors can also occur in a program if you have not considered all the details associated with the problem.

You can eliminate some of the errors if you carefully review your design and program before you enter it into the view window. Any remaining errors are resolved by editing the program. **Editing** is the process of entering and altering a program.

This section describes the most common types of editing. You will find the editing features of QuickBASIC to be both powerful and easy to use.

Deleting Previously Typed Characters   Use the arrow keys or mouse to position the cursor. Press the **Delete key** to delete the character under the cursor and the **Backspace key** to delete the character to the left of the cursor. To delete a series of adjacent characters in a line, position the cursor on the leftmost character to be deleted. Hold down one of the **Shift keys** and press the **Right Arrow key** until the characters to delete are highlighted. Press the **Delete key**.

If you have a mouse, select the adjacent characters to delete by moving the pointer from the first character to the last while holding down the mouse button.

Changing or Replacing Previously Typed Lines   Move the cursor to the character position where you want to make a change. Begin typing the new characters. QuickBASIC is by default in the insert mode. In the **insert mode**, the cursor is a blinking underline, and the character under the cursor and those to the right are *pushed* to the right as you enter new characters in the line. In the **overtype mode**, the cursor is a blinking box, and the character under the cursor is replaced by the one you type. Use the **Insert key** to toggle between the insert and overtype modes. As you enter new characters in this mode, they replace the old characters.

Adding New Lines   Press the **Enter key** to add a new or blank line. To add a new line above the current line, move the cursor to the first character and press the **Enter key**. To add a new line below the current line, move the cursor immediately to the right of the last character and press the **Enter key**.

You should only press the **Enter key** with the cursor at the beginning or end of a line. If you press the **Enter key** in the middle of a line, it is split. To join the split lines, press the **Backspace key** with the cursor on the first character of the second line.

Deleting A Series of Lines   Position the cursor at the beginning or end of the series of lines to delete. Hold down one of the **Shift keys** and press the **Up Arrow key** or **Down Arrow key** to highlight the series of lines. Press the **Delete key**.

If you have a mouse, highlight the lines to be deleted by holding down the mouse button and moving the pointer from the first character to the last in the series of lines. With the lines highlighted, press the **Delete key**.

Moving Text   Moving text from one location to another in a program is called **cut and paste**. To cut and paste text, follow these steps:

1. Use the arrow keys or mouse to move to the beginning of the text you want.
2. Hold down one of the **Shift keys** and use the arrow keys to select the text. If you are using a mouse, click the mouse button and move the pointer to select the text.
3. Hold down one of the **Shift keys** and press the **Delete key** to *cut* the text. The deleted text is placed in the clipboard. The **clipboard** is a temporary storage area that contains the last text deleted through the use of the **Shift key** and **Delete key**.
4. Move the cursor to the new location using the arrow keys or the mouse. Hold down one of the **Shift keys** and press the **Insert key** to *paste* the text.

Copying Lines   Copying text from one location to another in a program is called **pasting**. To paste text, follow these steps:

1. Use the arrow keys or mouse to move the cursor to the beginning of the text you want to paste.
2. Hold down one of the **Shift keys** and use the arrow keys to select the text. If you are using a mouse, hold down the mouse button and move the pointer to select the text.
3. Hold down the **Ctrl key** and press the **Insert key** to copy the text into the clipboard.
4. Move the cursor to the new location using the arrow keys or the mouse. Hold down one of the **Shift keys** and press the **Insert key** to *paste* the text.

You will find a summary of the editing keys on the last page of the reference card at the back of this book.

EXECUTING PROGRAMS AND HARD-COPY OUTPUT

The menu bar at the top of the screen contains eight menu names (Figure 1-19). Each menu name has a menu of commands. As we indicated earlier, to activate the menu bar, press the **Alt key**. Next, open a menu in one of two ways: (1) type the first letter in the menu name; or (2) use the **Left Arrow key** or **Right Arrow key** to move the cursor to the menu name and press the **Enter key**.

If you have a mouse, you can activate the menu bar and pull down a menu by moving the pointer to the menu name and clicking the mouse button.

The two most important menu names are Run and File. The **Run menu** is primarily used to execute the current program. The **File menu** contains several important commands. One in particular, the **Print** command, is used to print all or part of the current program.

Executing the Current Program

You execute (run) the current program by selecting the **Start** command in the **Run menu** (Figure 1-22 on the next page). The **Start** command can be selected in any one of the following three ways:

1. Press the **Alt key**, **R** for **Run**, and **S** for **Start**.

   or

2. Press **Shift + F5**.

   or

3. If you have a mouse, click on **Run** in the menu bar and click on **Start** in the Run menu.

If an error message displays within a dialog box when you execute the program, carefully read the message and then press the Enter key or click the OK button in the dialog box. QuickBASIC responds by highlighting the line with the error. Correct the line and execute the program again.

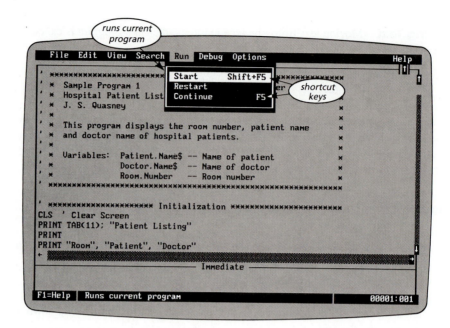

FIGURE 1-22
The Run menu

When the program first executes, QuickBASIC replaces the QB screen with the output screen. As we indicated earlier, the output screen shows the results due to the execution of the current program. Figure 1-23 shows the output screen for Sample Program 1. After you read the output results, you can redisplay the QB screen by pressing any key on the keyboard. This is indicated at the bottom of the output screen. To redisplay the output results, press the function key **F4**.

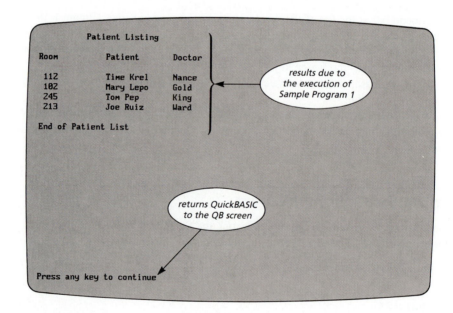

FIGURE 1-23
The output screen

Listing Program Lines to the Printer

Most programmers use a keyboard for input and a monitor (screen) for output. In many instances, it is desirable to list the program and the results on a printer. A listing of this type is called **hard-copy output**.

You can list all or part of the current program to the printer by using the **Print** command in the **File menu**. With the printer in the Ready mode, press the **Alt key** to activate the menu bar and type the letter **F** to pull down the **File menu** (Figure 1-24). Next, type the letter **P** for **Print** to print the current program. The three periods following the **Print** command mean a dialog box will appear requesting additional information. When the Print dialog box appears (Figure 1-25), make sure the bullet is next to the selection Current Module (Entire Program or Document if you are using the textbook version). Finally, press the **Enter key**.

If you have a mouse, click on **File**, click on **Print**, and click on **OK** when the Print dialog box appears.

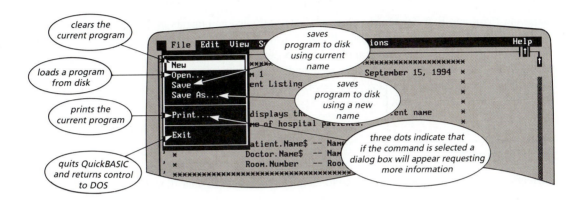

FIGURE 1-24 The File menu

Listing a Portion of the Program to the Printer

To print a portion of the current program, use the **Shift key** and arrow keys (or the mouse) to highlight the lines in the program you want to print. Next, follow the steps outlined in the previous paragraphs for printing the program. When the Print dialog box appears on the screen, the bullet should be in front of Selected Text (Figure 1-25). QuickBASIC automatically assigns the bullet to Selected Text when a series of lines is selected prior to issuing the **Print** command.

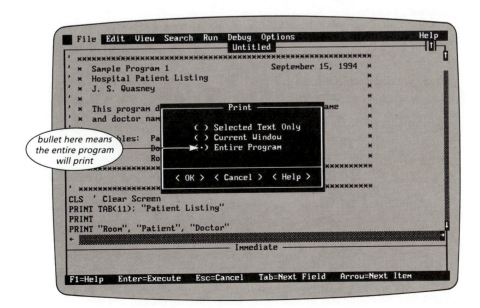

FIGURE 1-25 The dialog box for the Print command

Printing the Results on the Output Screen

To print a copy of the output screen, press **Print Screen** (**Shift + Prt Sc** on older PCs) while the output screen displays on the monitor. Later we discuss the LPRINT statement as an alternative means to generating hard-copy output.

SAVING, LOADING, AND ERASING PROGRAMS

Besides the **Print** and **Exit** commands, there are four additional commands in the **File menu** (Figure 1-24) that are essential for your first session with QuickBASIC—**Save**, **Save As**, **Open**, and **New**. The **Save** and **Save As** commands allow you to store the current program to disk. Later, you use the **Open** command to load the program from disk into main storage to make it the current one. The **New** command erases the current program from main memory. It clears the view window and indicates the beginning of a new program. Before we discuss these three commands further, it is important that you understand the concept of a file specification.

File Specifications

A **file specification**, also called a **filespec**, is used to identify programs and data files placed in auxiliary storage. A filespec is made up of a device name, file name, and extension.

$$\overbrace{\text{device name:file name.extension}}^{\text{filespec}}$$

The **device name** refers to the disk drive. If no device is specified, then the filespec refers to the default drive of the PC. If a device name is included in the filespec, then it must be followed by a colon.

File names can be from 1 to 8 characters in length. Valid characters are uppercase or lowercase A–Z, 0–9, and certain special characters ($ & # @ ! % " ( ) – { } _ / \). If an extension is used, then the file name must be followed by a period.

An **extension** that is up to three characters in length may be used to classify a file. Valid characters are the same as for a file name. With QuickBASIC, the default extension is bas. That is, when you use a command that requires a filespec, Quick-BASIC will automatically append an extension of bas if one is not included.

Examples of valid filespecs include b:payroll, b:lab2-1, PAYROLL.BAS, Accounts, and S123. The first two examples reference files on drive B. The latter three examples reference files on the default drive.

Saving the Current Program to Disk

When you enter a program through the keyboard, it is stored in main memory (RAM), and it displays in the view window. When you quit QuickBASIC or turn the computer off, the current program disappears from the screen and, more importantly, from main memory. To save a program to disk for later use, use the **Save** or **Save As** command in the **File menu**. Use the **Save** command to save the program under the same name. Use the **Save As** command to save the program under a new name. Because this is the first time we are saving the program, we will use the **Save As** command.

To select the **Save As** command, press the **Alt key** to activate the menu bar. Type the letter **F** to pull down the **File menu** (Figure 1-24). Type **A** for **Save As**. Here again, the three periods following the **Save As** command in the File menu mean QuickBASIC requires additional information. In this case QuickBASIC needs to know the filespec.

When the Save As dialog box appears (Figure 1-25), enter the file name and press the **Enter key**. In Figure 1-26, we entered the file name prg-1. QuickBASIC stores the current program using the filespec a:prg-1.bas. Notice in Figure 1-26 that the default drive (A:\) is specified below the file name box.

The **dirs/drives box** in the Save As dialog box includes a list of the disk drives and any subdirectories that are part of the current default drive. You may use the **Tab key** or mouse to activate this box and select a different default drive.

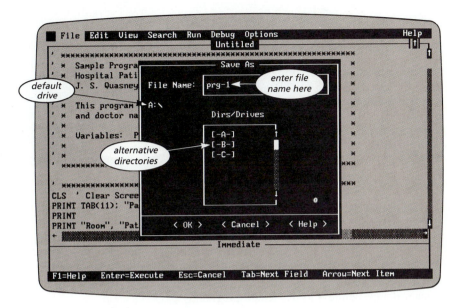

FIGURE 1-26   The dialog box for the Save As command

If you loaded the current program from disk or saved the program earlier, use the **Save** command to save the program under its current name.

To save the current program using a mouse, click on **File** and click on **Save** or **Save As**. If you click on **Save As**, enter the name in the file name box and click on the **OK** button.

Loading a Program from Disk

To load a program stored on disk into main storage, use the **Open** command in the **File menu** (Figure 1-24). This command causes the dialog box shown on the next page in Figure 1-27 to display. In the middle of the dialog box, QuickBASIC displays the files box. The **files box** lists the file names on the default drive that have an extension of bas. The current default drive displays just above the files box. To display any other directory on your PC, enter the disk drive (or path) in the file name box or select one from the dirs/drive box and press the **Enter key**.

In the file name box, enter the name of the program you want to load from auxiliary storage into main storage. In Figure 1-27 we entered the file name prg-1. Enter the file name by typing it on the keyboard or use the **Tab key** and arrow keys to select the file name from the file names box. Each time you press an arrow key, the name of the program under the cursor displays in the file names box. To complete the command, press the **Enter key**.

If you did not save the current program before attempting to load a new one, QuickBASIC will give you the opportunity to save it before it loads the new program into main storage.

To load a program from disk using the mouse, click on **File** and click on **Open**. Double-click on the name of the program in the files box.

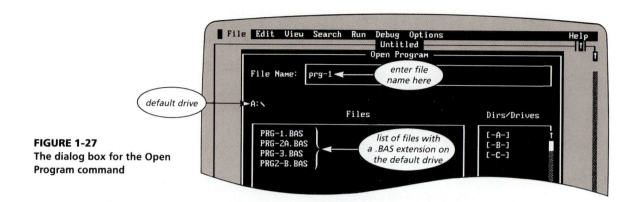

FIGURE 1-27
The dialog box for the Open Program command

Starting a New Program

The **New** command in the **File menu** (Figure 1-24) instructs QuickBASIC to erase the current program from main storage. This also clears the view window. Use this command when you are finished with the current program and wish to start a new one from scratch. Notice that it is not necessary to clear the current program if you are loading a program from disk. The **Open** command clears main storage before it loads the new program.

THE QB ADVISOR ON-LINE HELP SYSTEM

*T*he QB Advisor is a fully integrated, on-line help system with instant access to any QuickBASIC question. You can request immediate help when you first enter QuickBASIC by pressing the **Enter key** rather than the **Esc key**. Thereafter, at any time while you are using QuickBASIC, you can interact with the QB Advisor and display help screens on any QuickBASIC topic using the keys described on the last page of the reference card at the back of this book. For example, if you press **Shift + F1**, the initial help screen shown in Figure 1-28 displays. To return to the view window, press the **Esc key**. If you press **F1**, QuickBASIC displays help for the topic in which the cursor is positioned. The QB Advisor is literally a complete reference manual at your fingertips. The best way to familiarize yourself with the QB Advisor is to use it.

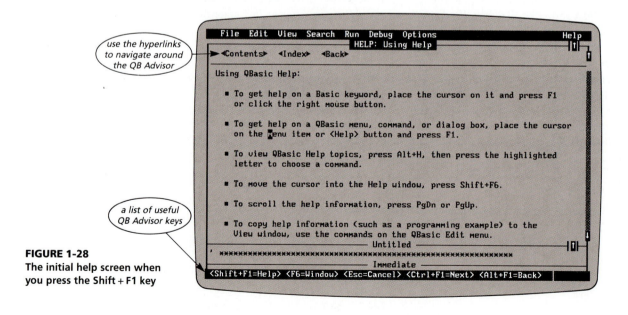

FIGURE 1-28
The initial help screen when you press the Shift + F1 key

TRY IT YOURSELF EXERCISES

1. Identify the 8 major components of the QB screen shown below.

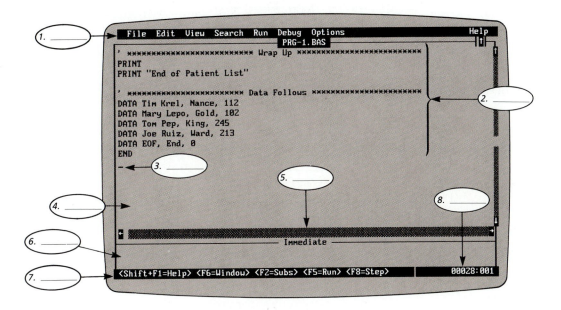

2. List the function of the following keys when a dialog box is active.
   a. Esc   b. Tab   c. Enter

3. List the function of the following keys when the view window is active.
   a. Alt   b. Shift + Delete   c. Enter
   d. Home   e. End   f. Ctrl + Home
   g. Ctrl + Q, X   h. Shift + F5   i. F4
   j. F6   k. Backspace   l. Delete
   m. Insert   n. Shift + Insert   o. Page Up

STUDENT ASSIGNMENTS

STUDENT ASSIGNMENT 1: Personnel Report

Instructions: Design and code a program using QuickBASIC to produce the personnel listing as shown on the next page under OUTPUT. The listing includes the employee name, department number, and pay rate for each employee shown under INPUT. Submit a program flowchart, listing of the program, and a listing of the output results. To obtain a hard copy of the output results, use the Print Screen key.

INPUT: Use the following sample data:

NAME	DEPT. NO.	PAY RATE
Sue Long	10	4.25
Chin Song	12	5.15
Mary Lopez	14	4.75
Jan Honig	14	3.85
EOF	99	9.99

Student Assignment 1 (continued)

OUTPUT: The following results are displayed:

```
              Personnel Report

   Dept.           Name           Pay Rate

    10            Sue Long          4.25
    12            Chin Song         5.15
    14            Mary Lopez        4.75
    14            Jan Honig         3.85

   End of Personnel Report
```

STUDENT ASSIGNMENT 2: Club Membership Report

Instructions: Design and code a program using QuickBASIC to produce the club membership listing shown under OUT-PUT. The listing includes a name, birth date, and age for each member shown under INPUT. Submit a program flowchart, listing of the program, and a listing of the output results. To obtain a hard copy of the output results, use the Print Screen key.

INPUT: Use the following sample data:

BIRTH DATE	AGE	NAME
December 7	41	John Sutherlin
March 16	38	Jim Wachtel
June 9	27	Mary Hathaway
August 6	25	Louise Scott
EOF	99	End

OUTPUT: The following results are displayed:

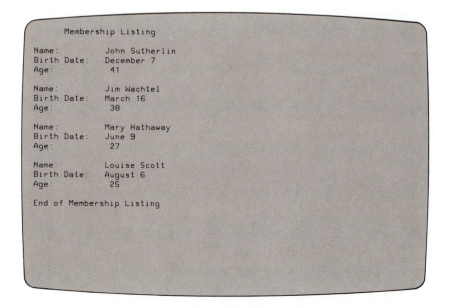

```
        Membership Listing

   Name:         John Sutherlin
   Birth Date:   December 7
   Age:             41

   Name:         Jim Wachtel
   Birth Date:   March 16
   Age:             38

   Name:         Mary Hathaway
   Birth Date:   June 9
   Age:             27

   Name:         Louise Scott
   Birth Date:   August 6
   Age:             25

   End of Membership Listing
```

PROJECT 2

Basic Arithmetic Operations and Accumulating Totals

Many applications require that arithmetic operations be performed on the input data to produce the required output. QuickBASIC includes the following basic arithmetic operators: addition (+), subtraction (–), multiplication (∗), division (/), and raising a value to a power (^). These operators are similar to those used in ordinary mathematics. The operators and an example of their use in a LET statement are illustrated in Figure 2-1.

MATHEMATICAL OPERATION	BASIC ARITHMETIC OPERATOR	EXAMPLE
Addition	+	LET Total = Sub1 + Sub2
Subtraction	–	LET Profit = Price - 5.95
Multiplication	∗	LET Gross = Hours ∗ Rate
Division	/	LET Amount = Cost / 5
Raising to a Power	^	LET Discount = Rate ^ 2

FIGURE 2-1 QuickBASIC arithmetic operators

THE LET STATEMENT

The LET statement is used to assign a variable a value. As shown in Figure 2-2, the first entry in a LET statement is the keyword LET. The keyword LET is followed by a variable name, an equal sign, and an expression.

> LET numeric variable = numeric expression
>
>   or
>
> LET string variable = string expression

FIGURE 2-2 The general form of the LET statement

Expressions

An **expression** can be numeric or string. A **numeric expression** consists of one or more numeric constants, numeric variables, and numeric function references, all of which are separated from each other by parentheses and arithmetic operators. A **string expression** consists of one or more string constants, string variables, and string functions separated by the concatenation operator (+), which combines two strings into one. A numeric expression can only be assigned to a numeric variable. A string expression can only be assigned to a string variable.

Figure 2-3 illustrates numeric expressions in LET statements. Figure 2-4 illustrates string expressions in LET statements.

VALUE OF	LET STATEMENT	RESULTS IN
A = 15 B = 10	LET F = A + B - 10	F = 15
J = 32 H = 16	LET L = J * 2 - H	L = 48
P = 14 Y = 7	LET Q = P / Y	Q = 2
W = 4 S = 6	LET T = 6 * (S - W)	T = 12

FIGURE 2-3   Numeric expressions in LET statements

VALUE OF	LET STATEMENT	RESULTS IN
X$ = ABC	LET W$ = "DEF" + X$	W$ = DEFABC
F$ = WATER G$ = WINE	LET A$ = F$ + " INTO " + G$	A$ = WATER INTO WINE
S$ = "TOP"	LET S$ = S$ + "IT"	S$ = TOPIT

FIGURE 2-4   String expressions in LET statements

From the examples in Figures 2-3 and 2-4 you can see that when performing arithmetic operations, the calculations are specified to the right of the equal sign. The variable assigned the result of the expression is placed to the left side of the equal sign.

Order of Operations

When multiple arithmetic operations are included in a LET statement, the **order of operations** follows the normal algebraic rules. That is, the operations are completed in the following order:

- First, exponentiation is performed from left to right.
- Next, multiplication and division are performed from left to right.
- Finally, addition and subtraction are performed from left to right.

For example, the expression $27 / 3 \wedge 2 + 4 * 3$ is evaluated as follows:

$$
\begin{aligned}
27 / 3 \wedge 2 + 4 * 3 &= 27 / 9 + 4 * 3 \\
&= 3 \qquad + 4 * 3 \\
&= 3 \qquad + 12 \\
&= 15
\end{aligned}
$$

If you had trouble following the logic behind this evaluation, use the following technique. Whenever a numeric expression is to be evaluated, *scan* from left to right three different times. On the first scan, every time you encounter an ^ operator, you perform exponentiation. In this example, 3 is raised to the power of 2, yielding 9.

On the second scan, moving from left to right again, every time you encounter the operators * and /, perform multiplication and division. Hence, 27 is divided by 9, yielding 3, and 4 and 3 are multiplied, yielding 12.

On the third scan, moving again from left to right, every time you detect the operators + and −, perform addition and subtraction. In this example, 3 and 12 are added to form 15. Thus, the following LET statement

```
LET Amount = 27 / 3 ^ 2 + 4 * 3
```

assigns 15 to the variable Amount.

The expression below yields the value of −19.37, as follows:

$$4 - 3 * 4 / 10 \char`^ 2 + 5 / 4 * 3 - 3 \char`^ 3 = 4 - 3 * 4 / 100 + 5 / 4 * 3 - 27$$
$$= 4 - 0.12 + 3.75 - 27$$
$$= -19.37$$

Hence, the following LET statement

```
LET Total = 4 - 3 * 4 / 10 ^ 2 + 5 / 4 * 3 - 3 ^ 3
```

assigns −19.37 to the variable Total.

The Use of Parentheses in an Expression

Parentheses may be used to change the order of operations. In QuickBASIC, parentheses are normally used to avoid ambiguity and to group terms in a numeric expression; they do not imply multiplication. When parentheses are inserted into an expression, the part of the expression within the parentheses is evaluated first, and then the remaining expression is evaluated according to the order of operations.

If the first example contained parentheses, as does (27 / 3) ^ 2 + 4 * 3, then it would be evaluated in the following manner:

$$(27 / 3) \char`^ 2 + 4 * 3 = 9 \char`^ 2 + 4 * 3$$
$$= 81 + 4 * 3$$
$$= 81 + 12$$
$$= 93$$

Use parentheses freely when you are in doubt as to the formation and evaluation of a numeric expression. For example, if you want to have the PC divide 9 * Tax by 3 ^ Payment, the expression may correctly be written as 9 * Tax / 3 ^ Payment, but you may also write it as (9 * Tax) / (3 ^ Payment) and feel more certain of the result.

For more complex expressions, QuickBASIC allows parentheses to be contained within other parentheses. When this occurs, the parentheses are said to be **nested**. In this case, QuickBASIC evaluates the innermost parenthetical expression first and then goes on to the outermost parenthetical expression. Thus, (27 / 3) ^ 2 + (5 * (7 + 3)) is broken down in the following manner:

$$(27 / 3) \char`^ 2 + (5 * (7 + 3)) = 9 \char`^ 2 + (5 * (7 + 3))$$
$$= 81 + (5 * 10)$$
$$= 81 + 50$$
$$= 131$$

SAMPLE PROGRAM 2 — AUTO EXPENSE REPORT

*T*he following sample program generates an auto expense report. The program performs calculations and accumulates totals using LET statements. Input consists of auto expense records that contain an employee name, the license number of the employee's car, the beginning mileage for the employee's car, and the ending mileage for the car.

The auto expense file that will be processed by the sample program is shown in Figure 2-5.

NAME	LICENSE	BEGINNING MILEAGE	ENDING MILEAGE
T. Rowe	HRT-111	19,100	19,224
R. Lopez	GLD-913	21,221	21,332
C. Deck	LIV-193	10,001	10,206
B. Alek	ZRT-904	15,957	16,419
EOF	End	0	0

FIGURE 2-5   The employee auto expense file for Sample Program 2

The output generated by Sample Program 2 is a report displayed on the screen. The report contains the employee name, the automobile license number, the total mileage, and the expense. The total mileage is calculated by subtracting the beginning mileage from the ending mileage. The expense is calculated by multiplying the mileage by twenty-five cents.

The report contains both report headings and column headings. After all records have been processed, the total number of employees and total auto expenses are displayed. In addition, the average expense per employee is calculated by dividing the total auto expense by the total number of employees. The average expense per employee is then displayed followed by an end-of-report message. The format of the output is shown in Figure 2-6.

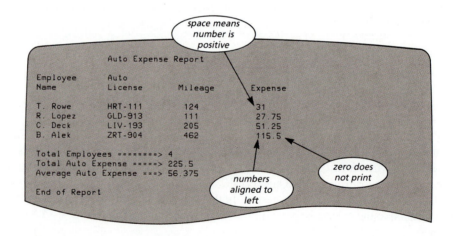

FIGURE 2-6
The report for Sample Program 2

When using the PRINT statement, nonsignificant zeros to the right of a decimal point are not printed. For example, Alek's expense displays as 115.5 rather than 115.50. In addition, when printing decimal numbers, the numbers are left aligned under the column heading rather than right aligned. The single space displayed to the left of each number means that the number is positive. These factors are illustrated in the output in Figure 2-6. Later in this section, we discuss the PRINT USING statement, which allows you to adjust the values displayed to include nonsignificant zeros and right-align numeric values under the column headings.

Accumulators

Most programs require **accumulators**, which are used to develop totals. Accumulators are initialized to a value of zero in the Initialization module, then incremented within the loop in the Process File module, and finally manipulated or displayed in the Wrap-Up module. Although QuickBASIC automatically initializes numeric variables to zero, good programming practice demands that this be done in the program. There are two types of accumulators: counters and running totals.

A **counter** is an accumulator that is used to count the number of times some action or event is performed. For example, appropriately placed within a loop, the statement

```
LET Total.Employees = Total.Employees + 1
```

causes the counter Total.Employees to increment by 1 each time a record is read. Associated with a counter is a statement placed in the Initialization module which initializes the counter to some value. In most cases the counter is initialized to zero.

A **running total** is an accumulator that is used to sum the different values that a variable is assigned during the execution of a program. For example, appropriately placed within a loop, the statement

```
LET Total.Expense = Total.Expense + Auto.Expense
```

causes Total.Expense to increase by the value of Auto.Expense. Total.Expense is called a running total. If a program is processing an employee file and the variable Auto.Expense is assigned the employee's auto expense each time a record is read, then variable Total.Expense represents the running total of the auto expense of all the employees in the file. As with a counter, a running total must be initialized to some predetermined value, such as zero, in the Initialization module.

Program Flowchart

The flowchart for the sample program, which produces an auto expense report and accumulates and prints final totals, is illustrated in Figure 2-7.

Prior to the loop in the flowchart, the accumulators are initialized, the headings are displayed, and the first employee record is read. Within the loop, the employee counter is incremented, the beginning mileage is subtracted from the ending mileage, giving the mileage driven by the employee. The auto expense is then calculated by multiplying the mileage driven times the auto cost per mile (.25). The auto expense is then added to the total auto expense accumulator. Next, a line of information is displayed. At the bottom of the loop another record is read. Control then returns to the top of the loop to determine if the trailer record was read. This looping process continues until there are no more auto expense records.

When the trailer record is read, the total number of employees and total auto expenses are displayed. Next, the total auto expense is divided by the total number of employees to give the average auto expense. Finally, the average and an end-of-report message are displayed.

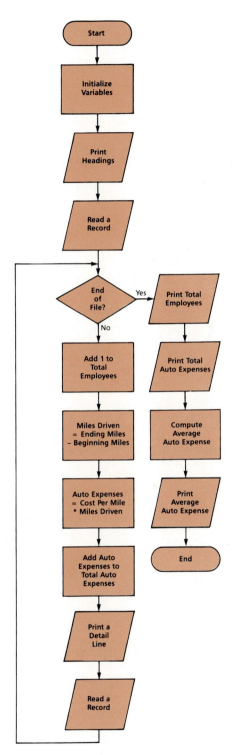

FIGURE 2-7 The flowchart for Sample Program 2

The QuickBASIC Program

The first section of the QuickBASIC program includes the initial documentation. As shown in Figure 2-8, the documentation is similar to Sample Program 1.

```
 1  ' *******************************************************************
 2  ' *  Sample Program 2                       September 15, 1994   *
 3  ' *  Auto Expense Report                                         *
 4  ' *  J. S. Quasney                                               *
 5  ' *                                                              *
 6  ' *  This program displays an auto expense report.  Mileage     *
 7  ' *  expense is calculated on the basis of 25 cents per mile.    *
 8  ' *  As part of the Wrap-Up module, the total number of          *
 9  ' *  employees, total auto expense, and the average expense      *
10  ' *  per employee are displayed.                                 *
11  ' *                                                              *
12  ' *  Variables:   Emp.Name$         -- Name of employee          *
13  ' *               License$          -- Auto license number       *
14  ' *               Begin.Mileage     -- Beginning mileage         *
15  ' *               End.Mileage       -- Ending mileage            *
16  ' *               Miles.Driven      -- Miles driven              *
17  ' *               Cost.Per.Mile     -- Auto cost per mile        *
18  ' *               Auto.Expense      -- Auto expense              *
19  ' *               Total.Employees   -- Number of employees       *
20  ' *               Total.Expense     -- Total auto expense        *
21  ' *               Average.Expense   -- Average auto expense      *
22  ' *******************************************************************
23
```

FIGURE 2-8
The initial documentation for Sample Program 2

The DATA Statements   The DATA statements in Figure 2-9 correspond to the employee auto expense file described in Figure 2-5.

```
55  ' ********************** Data Follows ***********************
56  DATA T. Rowe, HRT-111, 19100, 19224
57  DATA R. Lopez, GLD-913, 21221, 21332
58  DATA C. Deck, LIV-193, 10001, 10206
59  DATA B. Alek, ZRT-904, 15957, 16419
60  DATA EOF, End, 0, 0
61  END
```

FIGURE 2-9
The DATA statements for Sample Program 2

Initialization Module   Following the initial program documentation shown in Figure 2-8, the Initialization module initializes the accumulators to zero and displays the report title and column headings. The Initialization module is shown in Figure 2-10.

```
24  ' ******************** Initialization *********************
25  CLS  ' Clear Screen
26  LET Total.Employees = 0
27  LET Total.Expense = 0
28  LET Cost.Per.Mile = .25
29  PRINT TAB(15); "Auto Expense Report"
30  PRINT
31  PRINT "Employee", "Auto"
32  PRINT "Name", "License", "Mileage", "Expense"
33  PRINT
34
```

FIGURE 2-10
The Initialization module for Sample Program 2

Lines 26 and 27 initialize the employee counter (Total.Employees) and total expense running total (Total.Expense) to zero. When these two LET statements are executed, the zeros on the right side of the equal sign are assigned to the variables Total.Employee and Total.Expense. Counters and running totals should always be set to zero at the beginning of a program.

When the LET statement in line 28 is executed, the constant 0.25 on the right side of the equal sign is assigned to Cost.Per.Mile. This variable can then be used later to compute the auto expense. The purpose of assigning 0.25 to a variable is to facilitate future changes to the program. For example, if the auto cost per mile were changed from 0.25 to 0.28, the constant value in line 28 could be changed to 0.28.

Lines 29 through 33 display the report title and column headings. The PRINT statement in line 29 displays the report title beginning in column 15. Line 30 skips a line in the report. Lines 31 and 32 display the column headings. Finally, line 33 skips a line in the report to leave space between the column headings and the first record displayed.

The Process File Module   The statements that make up the Process File module for Sample Program 2 are illustrated in Figure 2-11.

```
35  ' ********************** Process File ***********************
36  READ Emp.Name$, License$, Begin.Mileage, End.Mileage
37  DO WHILE Emp.Name$ <> "EOF"
38     LET Total.Employees = Total.Employees + 1
39     LET Miles.Driven = End.Mileage - Begin.Mileage
40     LET Auto.Expense = Cost.Per.Mile * Miles.Driven
41     LET Total.Expense = Total.Expense + Auto.Expense
42     PRINT Emp.Name$, License$, Miles.Driven, Auto.Expense
43     READ Emp.Name$, License$, Begin.Mileage, End.Mileage
44  LOOP
45
```

FIGURE 2-11
The Process File module for
Sample Program 2

The READ statement in line 36 assigns the data in the first DATA statement (line 56 in Figure 2-9) to Emp.Name$, License$, Begin.Mileage, and End.Mileage. Next, the DO WHILE statement in line 37 tests to see if Emp.Name$ is not equal to EOF. Since Emp.Name$ does not equal EOF, control enters the loop.

The LET statement in line 38 increments the employee counter (Total.Employees). Each time this statement is executed, Total.Employees is incremented by 1. Since Total.Employees was initially set to zero (line 26 in Figure 2-10), it is equal to 1 after line 38 is executed the first time. After the statement is executed a second time, the value of Total.Employees is equal to 2. This counting continues each time through the loop. When the end-of-file is detected, the value of Total.Employees is equal to the number of records processed.

The LET statement in line 39 calculates the mileage the automobile was driven (Miles.Driven) by the employee being processed by subtracting the beginning mileage (Begin.Mileage) from the ending mileage (End.Mileage). Line 40 computes the auto expense (Auto.Expense) by multiplying the miles the automobile was driven (Miles.Driven) by the cost per mile (Cost.Per.Mile). The value 0.25 was assigned to Cost.Per.Mile in line 28 of the Initialization module (Figure 2-10).

The LET statement in line 41 adds the auto expense (Auto.Expense) to the accumulator Total.Expense. Here again, the variable Total.Expense was initialized to zero. When line 41 is executed the first time, the auto expense is added to the value zero. Hence, Auto.Expense is equal to the T. Rowe's auto expense after the first pass on the loop. When line 41 is executed the second time, the auto expense for R. Lopez is added to the auto expense for T. Rowe. Thus, the effect of this LET statement is to accumulate the auto expenses for all the employees.

The PRINT statement in line 42 displays the employee name, license number, miles driven, and the auto expense. Next, the READ statement in line 43 assigns the data for the second employee to Emp.Name$, License$, Begin.Mileage, and End.Mileage. The LOOP statement in line 44 transfers control back up to the DO WHILE statement in line 37. Notice that statements 38 through 43 are indented three spaces to illuminate the statements within the Do loop. The looping process continues until the trailer record is read, at which time control is transferred to the Wrap-Up module (line 47).

End-of-File Processing   After all the records are processed, control transfers to the PRINT statement in line 47 (Figure 2-12), which causes the PC to skip a line in the report. The next PRINT statement displays the total number of employees (Total.Employees). Notice the manner in which the PRINT statement is written to display both a constant and a variable. The phrase Total Employees ========> is enclosed within quotation marks (''). The right quotation is followed by a semicolon (;). A semicolon causes the PC to display the value of Total.Employees immediately after the phrase rather than in the next print zone. Recall that if the numeric value is positive, a blank space appears before the numeric value.

After line 49 displays the total expenses, line 50 computes the average expense which is displayed by line 51. Line 52 skips a line and line 53 displays an end-of-report message. Finally, line 61 (Figure 2-9) terminates execution of the program.

```
46  ' ************************* Wrap-Up *************************
47  PRINT
48  PRINT "Total Employees ========>"; Total.Employees
49  PRINT "Total Auto Expense =====>"; Total.Expense
50  LET Average.Expense = Total.Expense / Total.Employees
51  PRINT "Average Auto Expense ===>"; Average.Expense
52  PRINT
53  PRINT "End of Report"
54
```

FIGURE 2-12
The Wrap-Up module for
Sample Program 2

The Complete QuickBASIC Program   The complete Sample Program 2 is illustrated in Figure 2-13. The report generated by Sample Program 2 is shown in Figure 2-14.

```
1   ' *************************************************************
2   ' *  Sample Program 2                    September 15, 1994  *
3   ' *  Auto Expense Report                                     *
4   ' *  J. S. Quasney                                           *
5   ' *                                                          *
6   ' *  This program displays an auto expense report.  Mileage  *
7   ' *  expense is calculated on the basis of 25 cents per mile. *
8   ' *  As part of the Wrap-Up module, the total number of      *
9   ' *  employees, total auto expense, and the average expense  *
10  ' *  per employee are displayed.                             *
11  ' *                                                          *
12  ' *  Variables:   Emp.Name$        -- Name of employee        *
13  ' *               License$         -- Auto license number     *
14  ' *               Begin.Mileage    -- Beginning mileage       *
15  ' *               End.Mileage      -- Ending mileage          *
16  ' *               Miles.Driven     -- Miles driven            *
17  ' *               Cost.Per.Mile    -- Auto cost per mile      *
18  ' *               Auto.Expense     -- Auto expense            *
19  ' *               Total.Employees  -- Number of employees     *
20  ' *               Total.Expense    -- Total auto expense      *
21  ' *               Average.Expense  -- Average auto expense    *
22  ' *************************************************************
23
24  ' ******************** Initialization ********************
25  CLS  ' Clear Screen
26  LET Total.Employees = 0
27  LET Total.Expense = 0
28  LET Cost.Per.Mile = .25
29  PRINT TAB(15); "Auto Expense Report"
30  PRINT
31  PRINT "Employee", "Auto"
32  PRINT "Name", "License", "Mileage", "Expense"
33  PRINT
34
```

FIGURE 2-13
Sample Program 2

FIGURE 2-13
(continued)

```
35 ' ********************** Process File **********************
36 READ Emp.Name$, License$, Begin.Mileage, End.Mileage
37 DO WHILE Emp.Name$ <> "EOF"
38    LET Total.Employees = Total.Employees + 1
39    LET Miles.Driven = End.Mileage - Begin.Mileage
40    LET Auto.Expense = Cost.Per.Mile * Miles.Driven
41    LET Total.Expense = Total.Expense + Auto.Expense
42    PRINT Emp.Name$, License$, Miles.Driven, Auto.Expense
43    READ Emp.Name$, License$, Begin.Mileage, End.Mileage
44 LOOP
45
46 ' *********************** Wrap-Up ***********************
47 PRINT
48 PRINT "Total Employees =========>"; Total.Employees
49 PRINT "Total Auto Expense ======>"; Total.Expense
50 LET Average.Expense = Total.Expense / Total.Employees
51 PRINT "Average Auto Expense ===>"; Average.Expense
52 PRINT
53 PRINT "End of Report"
54
55 ' ********************** Data Follows **********************
56 DATA T. Rowe, HRT-111, 19100, 19224
57 DATA R. Lopez, GLD-913, 21221, 21332
58 DATA C. Deck, LIV-193, 10001, 10206
59 DATA B. Alek, ZRT-904, 15957, 16419
60 DATA EOF, End, 0, 0
61 END
```

```
                 Auto Expense Report

         Employee      Auto
         Name          License      Mileage      Expense

         T. Rowe       HRT-111       124          31
         R. Lopez      GLD-913       111          27.75
         C. Deck       LIV-193       205          51.25
         B. Alek       ZRT-904       462          115.5

         Total Employees =========> 4
         Total Auto Expense ======> 225.5
         Average Auto Expense ===> 56.375

         End of Report
```

FIGURE 2-14
The output results
due to the execution of
Sample Program 2

REPORT EDITING

Although the output in Figure 2-14 is readable, it does not conform to the format used by business and industry. For example, a column of numeric values usually has the decimal points aligned and is right-justified under the column heading. Numeric values that represent dollars and cents should include two digits to the right of the decimal point. Placing information in a format such as this is called **report editing**.

QuickBASIC provides for report editing through the use of the PRINT USING statement. This statement allows you to do the following:

- Specify the exact image of a line of output.
- Force decimal-point alignment when displaying numeric tables in columnar format.
- Control the number of digits displayed for a numeric result.

- Specify that commas be inserted into a number. (Starting from the units position of a number and progressing toward the left, digits are separated into groups of 3 by a comma.)
- Specify that the sign status of the number be displayed along with the number (+ or blank if positive, – if negative).
- Assign a fixed or floating dollar sign ($) to the number displayed.
- Force a numeric result to be displayed in exponential form.
- **Left-** or **right-justify** string values in a formatted field (that is, align the leftmost or rightmost characters, respectively).
- Specify that only the first character of a string be displayed.
- Round a value automatically to a specified number of decimal digits.

The general form of the PRINT USING statement is shown in Figure 2-15.

FIGURE 2-15
The general form of the PRINT USING statement

PRINT USING "format field"; list

or

PRINT USING string variable; list

where **format field** or **string variable** indicates the format and **list** is a variable or a group of variables separted by semicolons.

Report editing with the PRINT USING statement is accomplished using special characters to format the values to be displayed. When grouped together, these special characters form a **format field**. A format field is incorporated in a program as a string constant in the PRINT USING statement or as a string constant assigned to a string variable.

To illustrate the use of the PRINT USING statement, we will modify Sample Program 2. The new, formatted report is illustrated in Figure 2-16.

FIGURE 2-16
The formatted auto expense report

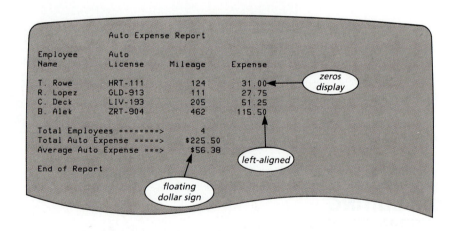

Compare the report in Figure 2-16 to the one in Figure 2-14. Notice that the mileage in the third column in Figure 2-16 is right-justified under the column heading. Also, the dollar and cents values in the expense field are right-justified under the column heading, and the decimal points are aligned. In addition, the total auto expense and the average expense per employee values are displayed with the dollar sign immediately adjacent to the leftmost digit in the number. This is known as a **floating dollar sign**.

To control the format of the displayed values, the PRINT USING statement is used in conjunction with a string expression that specifies exactly the image to which the output must conform. The string expression is placed immediately after the words PRINT USING in the form of a string constant or string variable. If the format is described by a string variable, then the string variable must be assigned the format by a LET statement before the PRINT USING statement is executed in the program. In either case, the items to display follow the string constant or string variable in the PRINT USING statement separated by semicolons or commas. The two methods for specifying the format for the PRINT USING statement are shown in Figure 2-17.

Method 1:

```
' Format Specified as a String in the PRINT USING Statement
PRINT USING "Item ### costs $$,###.##"; Item; Cost
```

Method 2:

```
' Format Specified Earlier and Assigned to a String Variable
D1$ = "Item ### cost $$,###.##"
    .
    .
    .
PRINT USING D1$; Item; Cost
```

FIGURE 2-17
The two methods for defining the format for a PRINT USING statement

In Method 1 of Figure 2-17, the string following the keywords PRINT USING instructs the PC to display the values of Item and Cost using the format found in the accompanying string constant. In Method 2, the string constant has been replaced by the string variable D1$ which was assigned the desired format in a previous statement. If Item is equal to 314 and Cost is equal to 2145.50, then the results displayed from the execution of either PRINT USING statement in Method 1 or Method 2 are as follows:

```
Item 314 costs $2,145.50
```

In Method 2 of Figure 2-17, notice that the keyword LET is not part of the LET statement. QuickBASIC considers any statement with an equal sign to be a LET statement. Hence, the keyword LET is optional. When defining format fields, we will not use the keyword LET.

Figure 2-18 illustrates how a LET statement and a PRINT USING statement are used to display the detail line in the report in Figure 2-16.

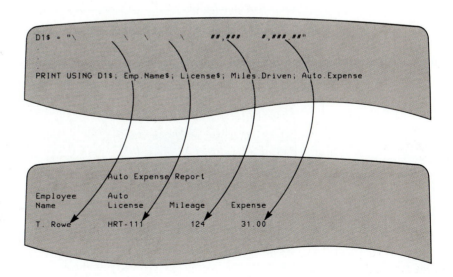

FIGURE 2-18
Using LET and PRINT USING statements to format the output

The backward slash (\) is used to create a format for string fields. The first backward slash indicates the first character position in the string field, and the second backward slash indicates the last character position in the field. Therefore, in the format field for Emp.Name$, eleven characters positions are defined—the two backward slashes and the nine spaces between them.

License$ is also a string variable. It is defined as eight characters in length by the two backward slashes and the six spaces between them. Numeric fields are defined through the use of the number sign (#). Each occurrence of a number sign corresponds to a numeric digit position. Punctuation, such as the comma and decimal point, is placed in the format field where it is to occur in the actual output. The format field for Miles.Driven includes a comma in case the value exceeds 999. Since Miles.Driven in the first line of the report is less than 1,000, the comma does not display. Similarly, a decimal point is placed in the format where it is supposed to print. For Auto.Expense, the format field ###.## specifies three digits to the left of the decimal point and two digits to the right of the decimal point. Thus, the value displays in dollars and cents form.

Notice in Figure 2-18, following the keyword PRINT USING, D1$ identifies the format. This variable name is then followed by a semicolon, and the names of the fields to display are separated by semicolons. The table in Figure 2-19 illustrates additional examples of format fields.

EXAMPLE	DATA	FORMAT FIELD	RESULTS IN
1	125.62	###.##	125.62
2	005.76	###.##	bb5.76
3	.65	###.##	bb0.65
4	1208.78	#,###.##	1,208.78
5	986.05	#,###.##	bb986.05
6	34.87	$$#,###.##	bbbb$34.87
7	3579.75	$$#,###.##	b$3,579.75
8	561.93	$##,###.##	$bbb561.93
9	SALLY	\ \	SALLY
10	EDWARD	\\	ED

FIGURE 2-19   **Examples of format fields (b represents a blank character)**

You can include constants in a format field. The LET statement in Figure 2-20 illustrates this point.

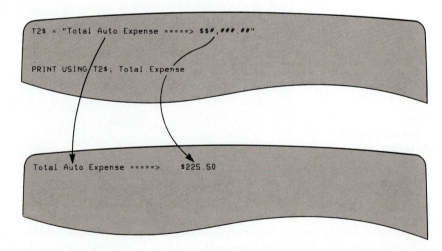

FIGURE 2-20
An example of including a constant in a format field

In Figure 2-20, the constant Total Auto Expense =====> is part of the string expression that includes the format field. When the variable T2$ is referenced by the PRINT USING statement, the constant is displayed exactly as it appears in the string expression. There are additional format symbols available with QuickBASIC. Those we present here, however, are the most widely used.

The coding in Figure 2-21 illustrates the complete program which produces the auto expense report shown on the next page in Figure 2-22. Particular attention should be paid to lines 30 through 39. These lines, when grouped together, show exactly what the report will look like when the program executes. Notice that this group of lines includes PRINT statements that display the report title and column headings and LET statements that define format fields. The column headings are within one string constant, rather than separated by commas, to better control the spacing. The format fields for the detail line (D1$) are immediately below the column headings in line 35.

We did not use the keyword LET in lines 35 through 39 so that all the string constants would begin in the same column in the program.

```
 1  ' *************************************************************
 2  ' *  Sample Program 2 Modified              September 15, 1994  *
 3  ' *  Auto Expense Report                                        *
 4  ' *  J. S. Quasney                                              *
 5  ' *                                                             *
 6  ' *  This program displays an auto expense report.  Mileage     *
 7  ' *  expense is calculated on the basis of 25 cents per mile.   *
 8  ' *  As part of the Wrap-Up module, the total number of         *
 9  ' *  employees, total auto expense, and the average expense     *
10  ' *  per employee are displayed.                                *
11  ' *                                                             *
12  ' *  Variables:  Emp.Name$         -- Name of employee          *
13  ' *              License$          -- Auto license number       *
14  ' *              Begin.Mileage     -- Beginning mileage         *
15  ' *              End.Mileage       -- Ending mileage            *
16  ' *              Miles.Driven      -- Miles driven              *
17  ' *              Cost.Per.Mile     -- Auto cost per mile        *
18  ' *              Auto.Expense      -- Auto expense              *
19  ' *              Total.Employees   -- Number of employees       *
20  ' *              Total.Expense     -- Total auto expense        *
21  ' *              Average.Expense   -- Average auto expense      *
22  ' *              D1$, T1$, T2$, T3$, T4$  --  Print images      *
23  ' *************************************************************
24
25  ' ******************** Initialization ********************
26  CLS   ' Clear Screen
27  LET Total.Employees = 0
28  LET Total.Expense = 0
29  LET Cost.Per.Mile = .25
30  PRINT "             Auto Expense Report"
31  PRINT
32  PRINT "Employee        Auto"
33  PRINT "Name           License      Mileage      Expense"
34  PRINT
35  D1$ = "\          \  \        \    ##,###      #,###.##"
36  T1$ = "Total Employees ========>    ###"
37  T2$ = "Total Auto Expense =====> $$#,###.##"
38  T3$ = "Average Auto Expense ===>  $$,###.##"
39  T4$ = "End of Report"
40
41  ' ******************** Process File ********************
42  READ Emp.Name$, License$, Begin.Mileage, End.Mileage
43  DO WHILE Emp.Name$ <> "EOF"
44     LET Total.Employees = Total.Employees + 1
45     LET Miles.Driven = End.Mileage - Begin.Mileage
46     LET Auto.Expense = Cost.Per.Mile * Miles.Driven
47     LET Total.Expense = Total.Expense + Auto.Expense
48     PRINT USING D1$; Emp.Name$; License$; Miles.Driven; Auto.Expense
49     READ Emp.Name$, License$, Begin.Mileage, End.Mileage
50  LOOP
51
```

image of report

FIGURE 2-21
Sample Program 2 modified
to include report editing

(continued)

FIGURE 2-21
(continued)

```
' ************************** Wrap Up **************************
PRINT
PRINT USING T1$; Total.Employees
PRINT USING T2$; Total.Expense
LET Average.Expense = Total.Expense / Total.Employees
PRINT USING T3$; Average.Expense
PRINT
PRINT T4$

' ************************ Data Follows ************************
DATA T. Rowe, HRT-111, 19100, 19224
DATA R. Lopez, GLD-913, 21221, 21332
DATA C. Deck, LIV-193, 10001, 10206
DATA B. Alek, ZRT-904, 15957, 16419
DATA EOF, End, 0, 0
END
```

```
               Auto Expense Report

Employee       Auto
Name           License      Mileage      Expense

T. Rowe        HRT-111          124        31.00
R. Lopez       GLD-913          111        27.75
C. Deck        LIV-193          205        51.25
B. Alek        ZRT-904          462       115.50

Total Employees ========>         4
Total Auto Expense =====>   $225.50
Average Auto Expense ===>    $56.38

End of Report
```

FIGURE 2-22
The formatted auto expense report due to the execution of the modified Sample Program 2

PRINTING A REPORT ON THE PRINTER

While the PRINT and PRINT USING statements display results on the screen, the LPRINT and LPRINT USING statements print results on the printer. Everything that has been presented with respect to the PRINT and PRINT USING statements in this section applies to the LPRINT and LPRINT USING statements. Obviously, to use these statements, you must have a printer attached to your PC and it must be in the Ready mode.

Figure 2-23 illustrates the results of the modified Sample Program 2 printed on a printer. To obtain the hard-copy results as shown in Figure 2-23, change all the PRINT and PRINT USING statements in Sample Program 2 (Figure 2-21) to LPRINT and LPRINT USING statements.

```
               Auto Expense Report

Employee       Auto
Name           License      Mileage      Expense

T. Rowe        HRT-111          124        31.00
R. Lopez       GLD-913          111        27.75
C. Deck        LIV-193          205        51.25
B. Alek        ZRT-904          462       115.50

Total Employees ========>         4
Total Auto Expense =====>   $225.50
Average Auto Expense ===>    $56.38
```

FIGURE 2-23
A printed version of the auto expense report

TRY IT YOURSELF EXERCISES

1. Which arithmetic operation is performed first in the following numeric expressions?

   a. `5 * (Amt + 8)`   b. `Cost - Sale + Discount`

   c. `8 / 3 * 5`   d. `(X * (2 + Y)) ^ 2 + Z ^ (2 ^ 2)`

   e. `X + Y / Z`

2. Evaluate each of the following:

   a. `2 * 10 * 6 / 12 - 7 ^ 2 / 7`

   b. `(6 - 8) + 5 ^ 3`

   c. `12 / 6 / 2 + 7 * 3 + 5`

3. Calculate the numeric value for each of the following valid numeric expressions if Amt = 3, Sale = 4, Cost = 5, Discount = 3, S1 = 4, S2 = 1 and S3 = 2.

   a. `(Amt + Sale / 2) + 6.2`

   b. `3 * (Amt ^ Sale) / Cost`

   c. `(Amt / (Cost + 1) * 4 - 5) / 2`

   d. `S2 + 2 * S3 * Discount / 3 - 7 / (S1 - S2 / S3) - Discount ^ S1`

4. Determine the output results for each of the following programs.

   a.
   ```
   ' Exercise 4.a
   X = 2.5
   Y = 4 * X / 2 * X + 10
   PRINT Y
   Y = 4 * X / (2 * X + 10)
   PRINT Y
   X = -X
   PRINT X
   X = -X
   PRINT X
   END
   ```

   b.
   ```
   ' Exercise 4.b
   C = 4
   D = 1
   S = C + D
   PRINT S
   T = D - C
   PRINT T
   C = S + T - C
   PRINT C
   D = 2 * (S + T + C) / 4
   PRINT D
   END
   ```

5. Calculate the numeric value for each of the following numeric expressions if X = 2, Y = 3, and Z = 6.

   a. `X + Y ^ 2`   b. `Z / Y / X`

   c. `12 / (3 + Z) - X`   d. `X ^ Y ^ Z`

   e. `X * Y + 2.5 * X + Z`   f. `(X ^ (2 + Y)) ^ 2 + Z ^ (2 ^ 2)`

6. Insert parentheses so that each of the following results in the value indicated on the right-hand side of the arrow.

   a. `10 / 3 + 2 + 12 ----> 14`

   b. `3 ^ 2 - 1 ----> 3`

   c. `6 / 2 + 1 + 3 * 4 ----> 4`

7. For each of the following format fields and corresponding data, indicate what the PC displays. Use the letter b to indicate the space character. Notice that if a format field does not include enough positions to the left of the decimal point, the PC displays the result preceded by a percent (%) sign. If the format field does not include enough positions to the right of the decimal point, the PC rounds the result to fit the format field.

Format Field	Data	Result
a. `####`	15	
b. `#,###`	345	
c. `$$,###.##`	1395.54	
d. `###.##`	12.5675	
e. `##,###.###`	19412.5	
f. `##.##`	576.3	
g. `###.#####`	32.2	
h. `#.##`	.234	

STUDENT ASSIGNMENTS

STUDENT ASSIGNMENT 1: Payroll Report

Instructions: Design and code a QuickBASIC program to generate the formatted payroll report shown under OUTPUT. The weekly pay is calculated by multiplying the hourly pay by the number of hours. All hours are paid at straight time. As part of the Wrap-Up module, display the total number of employees and the total weekly pay of all employees. Submit a program flowchart, listing of the program, and a listing of the output results.

INPUT: Use the following sample data:

EMPLOYEE NAME	HOURLY PAY RATE	HOURS WORKED
Joe Lomax	7.70	40
Ed Mann	6.05	38.5
Louis Orr	8.10	45
Ted Simms	9.50	39.5
Joan Zang	12.00	92
EOF	0	0

OUTPUT: The following results are displayed:

```
                    Payroll Report

Employee          Hourly        Hours         Weekly
Name              Rate          Worked        Pay

Joe Lomax          7.70          40.0          308.00
Ed Mann            6.05          38.5          232.93
Louis Orr          8.10          45.0          364.50
Ted Simms          9.50          39.5          375.25
Joan Zang         12.00          92.0        1,104.00

Total Employees ========>         5
Total Weekly Pay ========>    $2,384.68

End of Report
```

STUDENT ASSIGNMENT 2: Test Score Report

Instructions: Design and code a QuickBASIC program that prints the student test report shown under OUTPUT. In each detail line, include the student's name, test scores, and average test score. The average test score is calculated by adding the score for test 1 and the score for test 2 and dividing by 2. After all records for all students have been processed, print the total number of students and the class average for all tests. To obtain a class average, add all test scores and divide by twice the number of students. Use the LPRINT and LPRINT USING statements to generate the report on the printer.

INPUT: Use the following sample data:

STUDENT NAME	TEST 1 SCORE	TEST 2 SCORE
Julie Banks	70	78
John Davis	92	93
Joe Gomez	88	84
Sally Katz	78	83
EOF	0	0

OUTPUT: The following results are printed:

```
                Test Score Report

   Student
   Name          Test 1      Test 2     Average

   Julie Banks      70          78        74.0
   John Davis       92          93        92.5
   Joe Gomez        88          84        86.0
   Sally Katz       78          83        80.5

   Total Students ===========>    4
   Class Average  ===========>  83.25

   End of Report
```

PROJECT 3

Decisions

QuickBASIC includes the IF and SELECT CASE statements to instruct the PC to select one action or another on the basis of a comparison of numbers or strings. You use the IF statement to implement the **If-Then-Else structure** shown in Figure 3-1. When the structure in a flowchart has more than two alternative paths, you use the SELECT CASE statement. This type of structure is called a **case structure** and is shown in Figure 3-2.

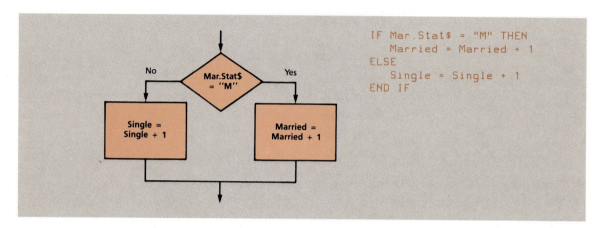

```
IF Mar.Stat$ = "M" THEN
    Married = Married + 1
ELSE
    Single = Single + 1
END IF
```

FIGURE 3-1   For the If-Then-Else structure, use the IF statement

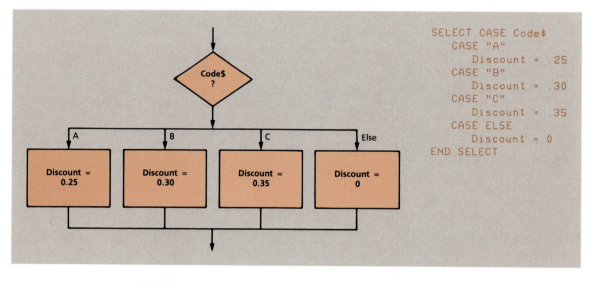

```
SELECT CASE Code$
    CASE "A"
        Discount = .25
    CASE "B"
        Discount = .30
    CASE "C"
        Discount = .35
    CASE ELSE
        Discount = 0
END SELECT
```

FIGURE 3-2   For a Case structure, use the SELECT CASE statement

THE IF STATEMENT

The IF statement is commonly regarded as the most powerful statement in QuickBASIC. The major function of this statement is to choose between two alternative paths. The IF statement has two general forms as shown in Figure 3-3.

Single-Line IF

IF condition THEN true task ELSE false task

Block IF

```
IF condition THEN
   true task
ELSE
   false task
END IF
```

FIGURE 3-3   The general form of the IF statement

In Figure 3-3, **condition** is a comparison between two expressions that is either true or false. **True task** and **false task** are statements or series of statements. If the condition is true, the PC executes the true task, also called the THEN clause, or **true case**. If the condition is false and an ELSE clause is included, the PC executes the false task, also called the ELSE clause, or **false case**. After either task is executed, control passes to the statement following the single-line IF statement or to the statement following the END IF for a block IF.

Figure 3-4 illustrates several examples of IF statements with conditions made up of numeric and string expressions. For numeric conditions, the PC evaluates not only the magnitude of each resultant expression but also its sign. For string expressions, the PC evaluates the two strings from left to right, one character at a time. With the block IF statement, the true and false tasks are indented by three spaces to improve the readability of the code.

Examples 1 through 3 in Figure 3-4 include conditions made up of numeric expressions. Examples 4 and 5 show IF statements with conditions made up of string expressions.

EXAMPLE	STATEMENT	VALUE OF VARIABLES	RESULT
1	`IF Amt = 0 THEN Dis = 4`	Amt = 0	The variable Dis is assigned the value 4, and control passes to the line following the IF statement.

2	`IF A < B THEN`
	`   PRINT X`
	`   T = T + 10`
	`ELSE`
	`   PRINT Y`
	`   Tax = Tax + 5`
	`END IF`
		A = 3
		B = 5
			The value of X is displayed; T is incremented by 10, and control passes to the line following the END IF.

3	`IF F < X - Y - 6 THEN`
	`   PRINT S`
	`END IF`
		F = 23
		X = 7
		Y = −8
			Control passes to the line following the END IF.

4	`IF C$ < D$ + E$ THEN`
	`   READ A, B, C`
	`   PRINT Y`
	`END IF`
		C$ = ''JIM''
		D$ = ''JA''
		E$ = ''MES''
			Control passes to the line following the END IF.

5	`IF X$ = "YES" THEN`
	`   PRINT A$`
	`END IF`
		X$ = ''yes''	Control passes to the line following the END IF. ''YES'' and ''yes'' are not the same string.

FIGURE 3-4   Examples of IF statements

Six types of relations can be used in a condition within an IF statement. These relations include determining if:

1. One value is equal to another (=)
2. One value is less than another (<)
3. One value is greater than another (>)
4. One value is less than or equal to another (< =)
5. One value is greater than or equal to another (> =)
6. One value is not equal to another (< >)

Recall that these are the same six relational operators we discussed earlier with the DO WHILE statement in Project 1 on page QB 9 in Figure 1-16.

CODING IF-THEN-ELSE STRUCTURES

his section describes various forms of the If-Then-Else structure and the use of IF statements to implement them in QuickBASIC.

Simple If-Then-Else Structures

Consider the If-Then-Else structure in Figure 3-5 and the corresponding methods of implementing the logic in QuickBASIC. Assume that the variable Age represents a person's age. If Age is greater than or equal to 18, the person is an adult. If Age is less than 18, the person is a minor. Adult and Minor are counters that are incremented as specified in the flowchart.

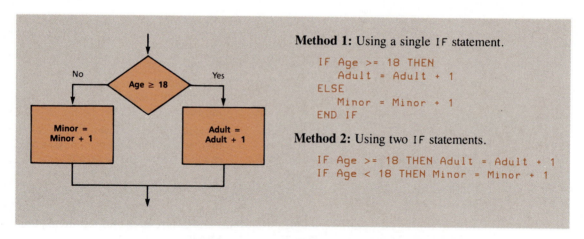

FIGURE 3-5   **Coding an If-Then-Else structure with alternative processing for the true and false cases**

In the first method shown in Figure 3-5, an IF statement resolves the logic indicated in the partial flowchart. The first line compares Age to 18. If Age is greater than or equal to 18, then Adult is incremented by 1. If Age is less than 18, the false task is carried out and Minor is incremented by 1. Regardless of the counter incremented, control passes to the statement following the END IF.

In Method 2, two single-line IF statements are used. Age is compared to the value 18 twice. In the first IF statement, the counter Adult is incremented by 1 if Age is greater than or equal to 18. In the second IF statement, the counter Minor is incremented by 1 if Age is less than 18.

Although both methods are valid and both satisfy the If-Then-Else structure, the first method is more efficient, as it involves fewer lines of code and less execution time. Therefore, the first method is recommended over the second.

Notice that the first method in Figure 3-5 could have been written as a single-line IF statement without the END IF. However, for readability purposes we recommend that you use the block IF statement as shown in Method 1.

As shown in Figures 3-6, 3-7, and 3-8, the If-Then-Else structure can take on a variety of appearances. In Figure 3-6, there is a task only if the condition is true.

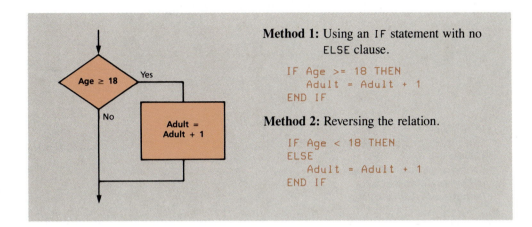

FIGURE 3-6
Coding an If-Then-Else structure with alternative processing for the true case

In Figure 3-6, the first method is preferred over the second since it is more straightforward and less confusing. In Method 2 of Figure 3-6, we reversed the relation. Although this method satisfies the If-Then-Else structure, it is also more difficult to understand. The second method shows that it is valid to have a null THEN clause.

The If-Then-Else structure in Figure 3-7 illustrates the incrementation of the counter Minor when the condition is false.

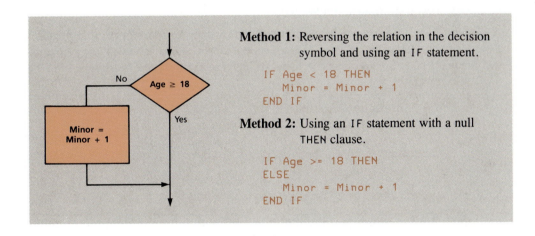

FIGURE 3-7
Coding an If-Then-Else structure with alternative processing for the false case

In Method 1, the relation in the condition that is found in the partial flowchart has been reversed. The condition Age >= 18 has been modified to read Age < 18 in the QuickBASIC code. Reversing the relation is usually preferred when additional tasks must be done as a result of the condition being false. In Method 2, the relation is the same as in the decision symbol. When the condition Age >= 18 is true, the null THEN clause simply passes control to the statement following the END IF. Either method is acceptable. Some programmers prefer always to include both a THEN and an ELSE clause, even when one of them is null. On the other hand, some prefer to reverse the relation rather than include a null clause.

On the next page in Figure 3-8, each task in the If-Then-Else structure is made up of multiple statements. We have included a suggested method of implementation.

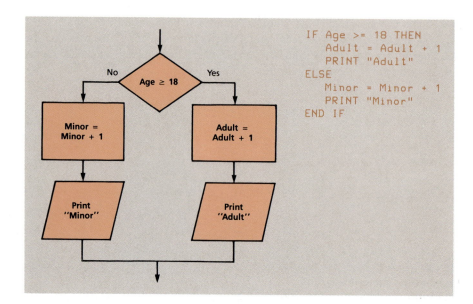

```
IF Age >= 18 THEN
    Adult = Adult + 1
    PRINT "Adult"
ELSE
    Minor = Minor + 1
    PRINT "Minor"
END IF
```

FIGURE 3-8
Coding an If-Then-Else structure with several statements for both the true and false cases

In the code in Figure 3-8, if the condition Age >= 18 is true, the two statements in the THEN clause are executed. If the condition is false, the two statements in the ELSE clause are executed.

Although there are alternative methods for implementing the If-Then-Else structure, the method we have presented is more straightforward and involves fewer lines of code.

Nested If-Then-Else Structures

A nested If-Then-Else structure is one in which the action to be taken for the true or false case includes yet another If-Then-Else structure. The second If-Then-Else structure is considered to be nested, or layered, within the first.

Study the partial program that corresponds to the nested If-Then-Else structure in Figure 3-9.

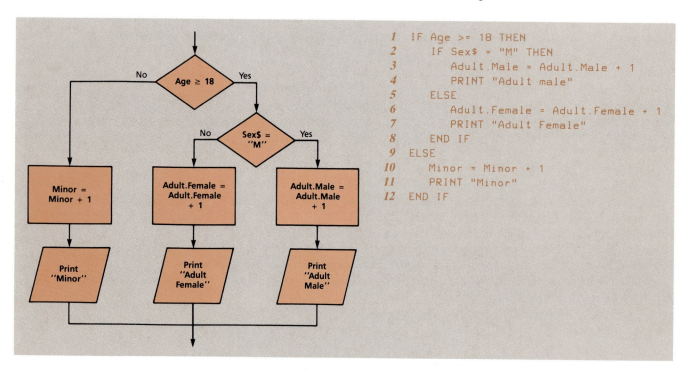

```
1  IF Age >= 18 THEN
2     IF Sex$ = "M" THEN
3        Adult.Male = Adult.Male + 1
4        PRINT "Adult male"
5     ELSE
6        Adult.Female = Adult.Female + 1
7        PRINT "Adult Female"
8     END IF
9  ELSE
10    Minor = Minor + 1
11    PRINT "Minor"
12 END IF
```

FIGURE 3-9   Coding a nested If-Then-Else structure

In the partial program in Figure 3-9, if the condition `Age >= 18` is true, control passes to the THEN clause beginning with line 2. If the condition is false, the ELSE clause beginning in line 10 is executed. If control does pass to line 2, then a second IF tests to determine if Sex$ equals the value M. If the condition in line 2 is true, lines 3 and 4 are executed. If the condition is false, then the PC executes lines 6 and 7.

QuickBASIC requires that you end each block IF statement with an END IF. Hence, the block IF in line 1 has a corresponding END IF in line 12, and the block IF in line 2 has a corresponding END IF in line 8.

Notice in Figure 3-9 that only one of the three alternative tasks is executed for each record processed. Regardless of the path taken, control eventually passes to the statement immediately following the last END IF in line 12.

SAMPLE PROGRAM 3 — VIDEO RENTAL REPORT

To illustrate a program that uses an IF statement, consider the following video rental problem. In this application, if the video tape is rented for three days or less, the charge is $2.49 per day. There is a one dollar per day discount for each of the first three days for customers who are at least 65 years old. If the video tape is rented for more than three days, the charge is $3.49 per day for each day over three days.

The video records consist of the customer's name, age, video title, and the number of days rented as shown in Figure 3-10.

CUSTOMER NAME	AGE	VIDEO TITLE	DAYS RENTED
Helen Moore	47	Lost in Space	1
Hank Fisher	67	Together Again	3
Joe Frank	34	Three Lives	7
Al Jones	64	The Last Day	5
Shirley Star	65	Monday Morning	4
EOF	0	End	0

FIGURE 3-10   The video rental file for Sample Program 3

The output is a printed video rental summary report that lists the customer name, customer age, title of the video tape rented, the number of days the tape was rented, and the charge for the rental. After all records have been processed, the number of senior citizen customers, the number of tapes rented, and the total charges are printed. The format of the output is illustrated in Figure 3-11.

```
                              Video Rental Report

        Customer                Video           Days
        Name            Age     Title           Rented   Charge

        Helen Moore     47      Lost in Space      1      2.49
        Hank Fisher     67      Together Again     3      4.47
        Joe Frank       34      Three Lives        7     21.43
        Al Jones        64      The Last Day       5     14.45
        Shirley Star    65      Monday Morning     4      7.96

        Senior Citizens ==========>      2
        Videos Rented   ==========>      5
        Total Charges   ==========>    $50.80

        End of Report
```

FIGURE 3-11   The report for Sample Program 3

Program Flowchart

The flowchart in Figure 3-12 illustrates the logic required to produce the video rental report.

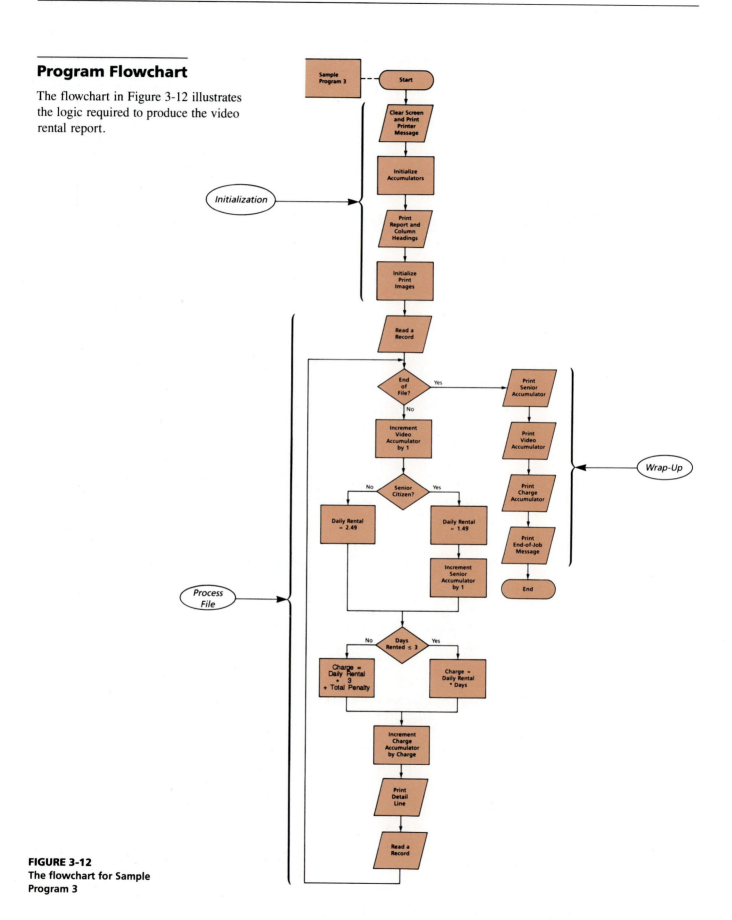

FIGURE 3-12
The flowchart for Sample Program 3

The QuickBASIC Program

The program in Figure 3-13 corresponds to the program flowchart in Figure 3-12.

FIGURE 3-13
Sample Program 3

```
1    '***********************************************************************
2    ' *   Sample Program 3                      September 15, 1994    *
3    ' *   Video Rental Report                                         *
4    ' *   J. S. Quasney                                               *
5    ' *                                                               *
6    ' *   This program prints a video rental report.  The charge      *
7    ' *   is based on the number of days the video is rented and      *
8    ' *   the age of the customer.                                    *
9    ' *        As part of the Wrap-Up module, the total number        *
10   ' *   of videos, senior customers, and charges are printed.       *
11   ' *                                                               *
12   ' *   Variables:   Cus.Name$         -- Name of customer           *
13   ' *               Cus.Age           -- Customer age               *
14   ' *               Video.Title$      -- Title of video             *
15   ' *               Days.Rented       -- Days rented                *
16   ' *               Daily.Rental      -- Cost per day               *
17   ' *               Charge            -- Cost of renting video      *
18   ' *               Penalty           -- Cost per day after 3 days  *
19   ' *               Total.Videos      -- Number of videos rented    *
20   ' *               Total.Seniors     -- Number of senior rentals   *
21   ' *               Total.Charges     -- Total charges              *
22   ' *               DL1$, TL1$, TL2$, TL3$, TL4$ -- Print images     *
23   '***********************************************************************
24
25   ' ********************** Initialization **********************
26   CLS   ' Clear Screen
27   PRINT "***** Video Rental Report Printing on Printer *****"
28   LET Total.Videos = 0
29   LET Total.Seniors = 0
30   LET Total.Charges = 0
31   LET Penalty = 3.49
32   LPRINT "                    Video Rental Report"
33   LPRINT
34   LPRINT "Customer                  Video                Days"
35   LPRINT "Name              Age     Title               Rented     Charge"
36   LPRINT
37   DL1$ = "\           \   ###    \              \        ###      ###.##"
38   TL1$ = "Senior Citizens ==========>    ###"
39   TL2$ = "Videos Rented ============>    ###"
40   TL3$ = "Total Charges ============> $$,###.##"
41   TL4$ = "End of Report"
42
```

(continued)

FIGURE 3-13
(continued)

```
43  ' *********************** Process File ***********************
44  READ Cus.Name$, Cus.Age, Video.Title$, Days.Rented
45  DO WHILE Cus.Name$ <> "EOF"
46     LET Total.Videos = Total.Videos + 1
47     IF Cus.Age >= 65 THEN
48        LET Daily.Rental = 1.49
49        LET Total.Seniors = Total.Seniors + 1
50     ELSE
51        LET Daily.Rental = 2.49
52     END IF
53     IF Days.Rented <= 3 THEN
54        LET Charge = Daily.Rental * Days.Rented
55     ELSE
56        LET Charge = (Daily.Rental * 3) + Penalty * (Days.Rented - 3)
57     END IF
58     LET Total.Charges = Total.Charges + Charge
59     LPRINT USING DL1$; Cus.Name$; Cus.Age; Video.Title$; Days.Rented; Charge
60     READ Cus.Name$, Cus.Age, Video.Title$, Days.Rented
61  LOOP
62
63  ' *********************** Wrap-Up ***********************
64  LPRINT
65  LPRINT USING TL1$; Total.Seniors
66  LPRINT USING TL2$; Total.Videos
67  LPRINT USING TL3$; Total.Charges
68  LPRINT
69  LPRINT TL4$
70
71  ' *********************** Data Follows ***********************
72  DATA Helen Moore, 47, Lost in Space, 1
73  DATA Hank Fisher, 67, Together Again, 3
74  DATA Joe Frank, 34, Three Lives, 7
75  DATA Al Jones, 64, The Last Day, 5
76  DATA Shirley Star, 65, Monday Morning, 4
77  DATA EOF, 0, End, 0
78  END
```

Discussion of Sample Program 3

When Sample Program 3 is executed, the report shown in Figure 3-14 prints on the printer. Sample Program 3 includes a few significant points that did not appear in previous programs. They are as follows:

- When executed, line 26 clears the screen and line 27 displays a friendly message informing the user that the report is being printed on the printer.
- LPRINT and LPRINT USING statements are used throughout the program to print the report on the printer rather than display the report on the monitor.
- There are two IF statements that select alternative paths on the basis of the data in the video record being processed. The block IF in lines 47 through 52 determines whether the customer is a senior citizen. If the customer is a senior citizen, the daily rental (Daily.Rental) is set to $1.49 and the senior citizen counter is incremented. If the customer is not a senior citizen, then the daily rental is set to $2.49.

The second block IF statement (lines 53 through 57) determines how much to charge the customer being processed. If the video is rented for three days or less, the charge is determined from the following LET statement:

```
LET Charge = Daily.Rental * Days.Rented
```

If the video is rented for more than three days, the charge is determined from the following LET statement:

```
LET Charge = (Daily.Rental * 3) + Penalty * (Days.Rented - 3)
```

```
                          Video Rental Report

         Customer                Video              Days
         Name           Age      Title              Rented    Charge

         Helen Moore    47       Lost in Space        1        2.49
         Hank Fisher    67       Together Again       3        4.47
         Joe Frank      34       Three Lives          7       21.43
         Al Jones       64       The Last Day         5       14.45
         Shirley Star   65       Monday Morning       4        7.96

         Senior Citizens ===========>        2
         Videos Rented ============>         5
         Total Charges ============>      $50.80

         End of Report
```

FIGURE 3-14
The report printed when
Sample Program 3 is executed

LOGICAL OPERATORS

In many instances, a decision to execute a true task or false task is based upon two or more conditions. In previous examples that involved two or more conditions, we tested each condition in a separate IF statement. In this section, we discuss combining conditions within one IF statement by means of the logical operators AND and OR. When two or more conditions are combined by these logical operators, the expression is called a **compound condition**. The logical operator NOT allows you to write a compound condition in which the truth value of the simple condition following NOT is **complemented**, or reversed.

The NOT Logical Operator

A simple condition that is preceded by the logical operator NOT forms a compound condition that is false when the simple condition is true. If the simple condition is false, then the compound condition is true. Consider the two IF statements in Figure 3-15. Both print the value of Discount if Margin is less than or equal to Cost.

Method 1: Using the NOT logical operator.

```
IF NOT Margin > Cost THEN
    PRINT Discount
END IF
```

Method 2: Reversing the relational operator.

```
IF Margin <= Cost THEN
    PRINT Discount
END IF
```

FIGURE 3-15
Use of the NOT logical operator

In Method 1 of Figure 3-15, if Margin is greater than Cost (the simple condition is true), then the compound condition NOT Margin > Cost is false. If Margin is less than or equal to Cost (the simple condition is false), then the NOT makes the compound condition true. In Method 2, the relational operator is reversed and, therefore, the NOT is eliminated. Both methods are equivalent.

Because the logical operator NOT can increase the complexity of the decision statement significantly, use it sparingly. As shown in Figure 3-15, you can always reverse the relational operator in a condition to eliminate the logical operator NOT.

The AND Logical Operator

The AND operator requires that both conditions be true for the compound condition to be true. Consider the two IF statements in Figure 3-16. Both methods read a value for Selling.Price if Margin is greater than 10 and Cost is less than 8.

Method 1: Using the AND logical operator.

```
IF Margin > 10 AND Cost < 8 THEN
    READ Selling.Price
END IF
```

Method 2: Using nested IF statements.

```
IF Margin > 10 THEN
    IF Cost < 8 THEN
        READ Selling.Price
    END IF
END IF
```

FIGURE 3-16   Use of the AND operator

In Method 1 of Figure 3-16, if Margin is greater than 10 and Cost is less than 8, the READ statement assigns a value to Selling.Price before control passes to the line following the END IF. If either one of the conditions is false, then the compound condition is false, and control passes to the line following the END IF without a value being read for Selling.Price. Although both methods are equivalent, Method 1 is more efficient, more compact, and more straightforward than Method 2.

Like a single condition, a compound condition can be only true or false. To determine the truth value of the compound condition, the PC must evaluate and assign a truth value to each individual condition. Then the truth value is determined for the compound condition.

For example, if A equals 4 and C$ equals "X", the PC evaluates the following compound condition in the manner shown:

```
IF A = 3 AND C$ = "X" THEN LET F = F + 1
   ‾‾‾‾‾       ‾‾‾‾‾‾‾‾
   1. false    2. true
        ‾‾‾‾‾‾‾‾‾‾‾‾‾‾
        3. false
```

The PC first determines the truth value for each condition, then concludes that the compound condition is false because of the AND operator.

The OR Logical Operator

The OR operator requires that only one of the two conditions be true for the compound condition to be true. If both conditions are true, the compound condition is also true. Likewise, if both conditions are false, the compound condition is false. The use of the OR operator is illustrated in Figure 3-17.

Method 1: Using the OR logical operator.

```
IF Code$ = "A" OR Marital.Status$ = "M" THEN
    END
END IF
```

Method 2: Using two IF statements.

```
IF Code$ = "A" THEN
    END
END IF
IF Marital.Status$ = "M" THEN
    END
END IF
```

FIGURE 3-17   Use of the OR operator

In Method 1 of Figure 3-17, if either Code$ equals the value A or Marital.Status$ equals the value M, the THEN clause is executed and the program halts execution. If both conditions are true, the THEN clause is also executed. If both conditions are false, the THEN clause is bypassed, and control passes to the line following the END IF. Method 2 employs two IF statements to resolve the same If-Then-Else structure. Again, both methods are equivalent, but, Method 1 is easier to read and understand than Method 2.

As with the logical operator AND, the truth values of the individual conditions in the IF statement are first determined, then the truth values for the conditions containing the logical operator OR are evaluated. For example, if F equals 4 and H equals 5, the following condition is true:

```
IF F = 3 OR H = 5 THEN PRINT "Yes"
     1. false    2. true
           3. true
```

Combining Logical Operators

Logical operators can be combined in a decision statement to form a compound condition. The formation of compound statements that involve more than one type of logical operator can create problems unless you fully understand the order in which the PC evaluates the entire condition. Unless parentheses dictate otherwise, reading from left to right, conditions containing arithmetic operators are evaluated first; then those containing relational operators; then those containing NOT operators; then those containing AND operators; then those containing OR operators. Refer to the last page of the Reference Card at the back of this book for a summary listing of the order of both arithmetic and logical operators.

For the following compound condition assume, that D = 3, P = 5, R = 3, T = 5, S = 6, and Y = 3:

```
IF S > Y  OR  T = D  AND  P < 5  OR  NOT Y = R  THEN READ L
   1. true      2. false      3. false       4. true
                6. false                      5. false
        7. true
                          8. true
```

The Use of Parentheses in Compound Conditions

Parentheses may be used to change the order of precedence. When there are parentheses in a compound condition, the PC evaluates that part of the compound condition within the parentheses first, then continues to evaluate the remaining compound condition according to the order of logical operations. For example, suppose variable J has a value of 2, and E has a value of 6. Consider the following compound condition:

```
IF  J = 7  AND  E > 5   OR   J <> 0  THEN LET Cnt = Cnt + 1
    1. false     2. true       3. true
          4. false
                5. true
```

Following the order of logical operations, the compound condition yields a truth value of true. If parentheses surround the last two conditions, then the OR operator is evaluated before the AND condition, and the compound condition yields a truth value of false, as shown:

```
IF  J = 7  AND  (E > 5   OR   J <> 0)  THEN LET Cnt = Cnt + 1
    4. false      1. true       2. true
                     3. true
             5. false
```

Parentheses may be used freely when the evaluation of a compound condition is in doubt. For example, if you wish to evaluate the compound condition

```
IF C > D AND S = 4 OR X < Y AND T = 5 THEN READ F
```

you may incorporate it into a decision statement as it stands. You may also write in the following way:

```
IF (C > D AND S = 4) OR (X < Y AND T = 5) THEN READ F
```

and feel more certain of the outcome of the decision statement.

THE SELECT CASE STATEMENT

*T*he SELECT CASE statement is used to implement the case structure. Figure 3-18 illustrates the implementation of a case structure, which determines a letter grade (Letter.Grade$) from a grade point average (GPA) using the following grading scale:

GRADE POINT AVERAGE	LETTER GRADE
$GPA \geq 90$	A
$80 \leq GPA < 90$	B
$70 \leq GPA < 80$	C
$60 \leq GPA < 70$	D
$0 \leq GPA < 60$	F
$GPA < 0$	Error

For example, if your GPA is 79.6, your letter grade is a C.

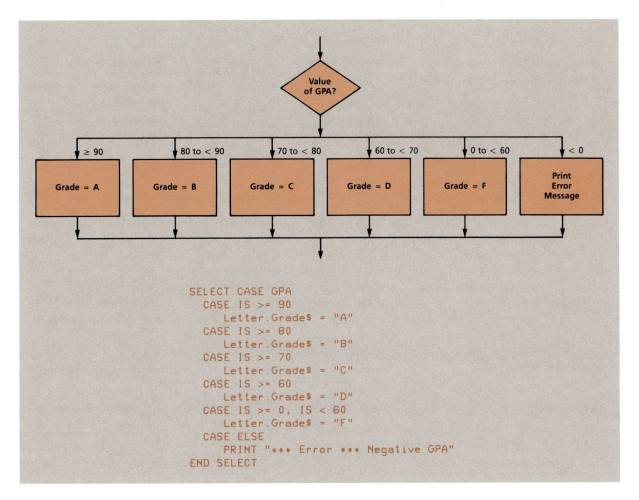

FIGURE 3-18   Implementation of a case structure

The SELECT CASE statement in Figure 3-18 is used to implement the grading scale. When the PC executes the SELECT CASE statement, it compares the variable GPA, which follows the keywords SELECT CASE, to the expressions following the keyword CASE in each CASE clause, also called a **case**. The PC begins the comparison with the first case and continues through the remaining ones until it finds a match. When a match is found, the range of statements immediately following the keyword CASE is executed. Following execution of the case, control immediately transfers to the statement following the END SELECT. The PC does not search for additional matches in the remaining cases.

For example, if GPA is equal to 79.6, then the PC finds a match in the third case. Therefore, it assigns Letter.Grade$ the value C and passes control to the statement following the END SELECT. If GPA equals a negative value, then no match is found, and the PRINT statement following the CASE ELSE is executed.

The CASE ELSE just prior to the END SELECT in Figure 3-18 instructs the PC to use this case if there is no match with any of the previous CASE clauses.

In a SELECT CASE, you place the variable, or expression, also called the **test-expression**, to test after the keywords SELECT CASE. Next, you assign the group of values, also called the **match-expression**, that make each alternative case true after the keyword CASE. Each case contains the range of statements to execute, and you may have as many cases as required. After the last case, end the SELECT CASE with an END SELECT.

The general form of the SELECT CASE statement is shown in Figure 3-19.

```
SELECT CASE test-expression
   CASE match-expression
        [range of statements]
   CASE match-expression
        [range of statements]
        .
        .
        .
   CASE ELSE
        [range of statements]
END SELECT
```

where **test-expression** is a numeric or string expression and **match-expression** indicates the values for which the case is selected.

FIGURE 3-19   The general form of the SELECT CASE statement

Valid Match-Expressions

There are several ways to construct valid match-expressions following the keyword CASE. Consider the match-expressions in Figure 3-20.

EXAMPLE	MATCH-EXPRESSION
1	CASE "F" TO "H", "S", Code$
2	CASE IS = Salary, IS = Max.Salary - 5000
3	CASE IS < 12, 20 TO 30, 48.6, IS > 100

FIGURE 3-20   Valid match-expressions in a SELECT CASE statement

In Example 1 in Figure 3-20, the match-expression is a list made up of the letters F to H, the letter S, and the value of the variable Code$. In Example 2, the match-expression includes Salary and the expression Max.Salary – 5000. If a relational operator is used, then the keyword IS is required. The second value in the list of Example 2 shows that expressions with arithmetic operators are allowed. The third example includes a list that requires the use of the keywords IS and TO. Use the keyword IS before any relational operator, such as = or >. Use the keyword TO to define a range of values.

TRY IT YOURSELF EXERCISES

1. Determine the value of Amt that will cause the condition in the following IF statements to be true:
   a. IF Amt > 8 OR Amt = 3 THEN
         Z = Z / 10
      END IF
   b. IF Amt + 10 >= 7 AND NOT Amt < 0 THEN
         PRINT "The answer is"; A
      END IF

2. Construct partial programs for each of these structures.

a.

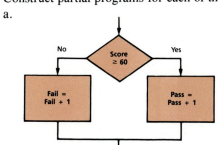

b.

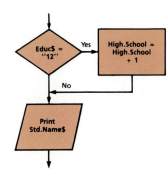

3. Construct partial programs for each of these logic structures.

a.

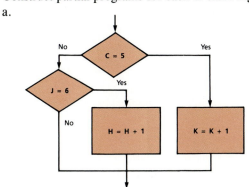

b.

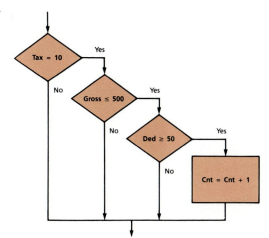

4. What is displayed if the following program is executed?

```
' Exercise 4
READ I
DO WHILE I <> -99
    SELECT CASE I
        CASE 1, 4, 7
            PRINT I, "Case 1"
        CASE IS < 8
            PRINT I, "Case 2"
        CASE 14 TO 21
            PRINT I, "Case 3"
        CASE ELSE
            PRINT I, "Case 4"
    END SELECT
    READ I
LOOP
DATA 1, 4, 7, 2, 21, 20, -99
END
```

5. Given the following:

Emp.Num = 500
Salary = $700
Job.Code$ = "1"
Tax = $60
Insurance.Ded = $40

Determine the truth value of the following compound conditions:

a. `Emp.Num < 400 OR Job.Code$ = "1"`
b. `Salary = 700 AND Tax = 50`
c. `Salary - Tax = 640 AND Job.Code$ = "1"`
d. `Tax + Insurance.Ded = Salary - 500 OR Job.Code$ = "0"`
e. `NOT Job.Code$ < "0"`
f. `NOT (Job.Code$ = "1" OR Tax = 60)`
g. `Salary < 300 AND Insurance.Ded < 50 OR Job.Code$ = "1"`
h. `Salary < 300 AND (Insurance.Ded < 50 OR Job.Code$ = "1")`
i. `NOT (NOT Job.Code$ = "1")`

6. Given the following:

$T = 0$, $V = 4$, $B = 7$, $Y = 8$, and $X = 3$

Determine the action taken for each of the following:

a.
```
IF T > 0 THEN
     READ A
END IF
```
b.
```
IF B = 4 OR T > 7 THEN
     IF X > 1 THEN
          READ A
     END IF
END IF
```
c.
```
IF X = 3 OR T > 2 THEN
     IF Y > 7 THEN
          READ A
     END IF
END IF
```
d.
```
IF X + 2 < 5 THEN
     IF B < V + X THEN
          READ A
     END IF
END IF
```

7. Write a program that determines the number of negative values (Negative), number of zero values (Zero) and number of positive values (Positive) in the following data set: 4, 2, 3, –9, 0, 0, –4, –6, –8, 3, 2, 0, 0, 8, –3, 4. Use the –999999 to test for the end-of-file.

8. The values of three variables Num1, Num2, and Num3 are positive and not equal to each other. Using `IF` statements, determine which has the smallest value and assign this value to Little.

9. The IOU National Bank computes its monthly service charge on checking accounts by adding $0.50 to a value computed from the following:

$0.21 per check for the first ten checks
$0.19 per check for the next ten checks
$0.17 per check for the next ten checks
$0.15 per check for the remaining checks

Write a sequence of statements that includes a `SELECT CASE` statement and a `PRINT` statement to display the account number (Account), the number of checks cashed (Checks), and the computed monthly charge (Charge). Assume the account number and the number of checks cashed are in `DATA` statements.

STUDENT ASSIGNMENTS

STUDENT ASSIGNMENT 1: Student Registration Report

Instructions: Design and code a QuickBASIC program to process the data shown under INPUT. Generate the student registration report shown under OUTPUT. A student with less than 12 hours is defined as part-time. The registration fee is determined from the following:

Credits Hours	Fee
Less than 12	$400.00
12 or more	$400.00 plus $30.00 per credit hour in excess of 11 hours

As part of the end-of-job routine, print the total number of part-time students, full-time students, students, and fees.

INPUT: Use the following sample data:

STUDENT NAME	CREDIT HOURS
Joe Franks	14
Ed Crane	9
Susan Lewis	18
Fred Smith	12
Jack North	10
Nikole Hiegh	17
EOF	0

OUTPUT: The following results are printed:

```
            Student Registration

   Student        Credit
   Name           Hours        Fee      Status

   Joe Franks       14       490.00     Full-Time
   Ed Crane          9       400.00     Part-Time
   Susan Lewis      18       610.00     Full-Time
   Fred Smith       12       430.00     Full-Time
   Jack North       10       400.00     Part-Time
   Nikole Hiegh     17       580.00     Full-Time

   Total Part-Time ====>        2
   Total Full-Time ====>        4
   Total Students  =====>       6
   Total Fees =========>  $2,910.00

   End of Report
```

STUDENT ASSIGNMENT 2: Employee Salary Increase Report

Instructions: Design and code a QuickBASIC program to process the data shown under INPUT. Use IF statements with compound conditions to display on the screen the employee salary increase report shown under OUTPUT.

Determine the employee salary increase from the following:

1. All employees get a 4% salary increase
2. All employees get a 0.025% times the number of annual merits salary increase.
3. Employees with more than three annual merits and 10 or more years of service get an additional 2.5% salary increase
4. Employees with four or more annual merits and less than 10 years of service get an additional 1.5% salary increase

INPUT: Use the following sample data. Make sure you enclose the employee names within quotation marks, since each name includes a comma.

EMPLOYEE NAME	ANNUAL MERITS	SERVICE	CURRENT SALARY
Babjack, Bill	9	3	$19,500
Knopf, Louis	0	19	29,200
Taylor, Jane	8	12	26,000
Droopey, Joe	8	4	28,000
Lane, Lyn	2	9	19,800
Lis, Frank	6	1	21,000
Lopez, Hector	10	1	15,000
Braion, Jim	8	19	26,500
EOF	0	0	0

OUTPUT: The following results are displayed:

```
               Employee Salary Increase Report

Employee        Annual     Current                  New
Name            Merits     Salary        Raise      Salary

Babjack, Bill     9        19,500.00    1,116.38    20,616.38
Knopf, Louis      0        29,200.00    1,168.00    30,368.00
Taylor, Jane      8        26,000.00    1,742.00    27,742.00
Droopey, Joe      8        28,000.00    1,596.00    29,596.00
Lane, Lyn         2        19,800.00      801.90    20,601.90
Lis, Frank        6        21,000.00    1,186.50    22,186.50
Lopez, Hector    10        15,000.00      862.50    15,862.50
Braion, Jim       8        26,500.00    1,775.50    28,275.50
                          ==========   ========   ==========
                         185,000.00   10,248.78   195,248.78

Total Employees ============>       8
Average Employee Raise ======>  $1,281.10

End of Report
```

STUDENT ASSIGNMENT 3: Computer Usage Report

Instructions: Design and code a QuickBASIC program to process the data shown under INPUT and prints the report shown under OUTPUT. Use the SELECT CASE statement to determine the computer charges. At the end-of-job, print the total customers, total hours in decimal, and the total charges. The monthly charges can be determined from the following:
1. $165.00 for one hour or less usage
2. $240.00 for usage greater than one hour and less than or equal to two hours
3. $300.00 for usage greater than two hours and less than or equal to three hours
4. $330.00 for usage greater than three hours and less than or equal to four hours
5. $375.00 for usage greater than four hours and less than or equal to five hours
6. $1.25 per minute if the usage is greater than five hours

INPUT: Use the following sample data:

CUSTOMER NAME	HOURS	MINUTES
Acme Inc.	2	0
Hitek	2	50
Floline	5	10
Niki's Food	1	14
Amanda Inc.	6	22
EOF	0	0

OUTPUT: The following results are printed:

```
              Computer Usage Report

   Customer
   Name          Hours      Minutes     Charges

   Acme Inc.       2            0        240.00
   Hitek           2           50        300.00
   Floline         5           10        387.50
   Niki's Food     1           14        240.00
   Amanda Inc.     6           22        477.50

   Total Customers ========>        5
   Total Hours ===========>        17.60
   Total Charges ==========>    $1,645.00

   End of Report
```

PROJECT 4

Interactive Programming, For Loops, and an Introduction to the Top-Down Approach

One of the major tasks of any program is to integrate the data that is to be processed into the program. In the first three projects, the READ and DATA statements were used to integrate the data into the program. This project introduces you to another method of data integration through the use of the INPUT statement. The INPUT statement is different than the READ and DATA statements, because with the INPUT statement the data is entered *during* execution rather than as *part of the program.*

A second topic covered in this project is alternative methods for implementing loops in QuickBASIC. Through the first three projects, we have consistently created loops using the DO WHILE and LOOP statements. In this project we discuss the creation of loops using the DO and LOOP UNTIL statements and the FOR and NEXT statements. The DO and LOOP UNTIL statements allow you to create loops that test for termination at the bottom of the loop rather than at the top of the loop. The FOR and NEXT statements allow you to more efficiently establish counter-controlled loops. A **counter-controlled loop** is one that exits the loop when a counter has reached a specified number.

Finally, this project presents the top-down approach to solving problems. The top-down approach is a useful methodology for solving large and complex problems. This approach breaks the problem into smaller parts and allows you to solve each part independent of the others.

THE INPUT STATEMENT

The INPUT statement causes a program to temporarily halt execution and accept data through the keyboard as shown in Figure 4-1. After the user enters the required data (1.25 in Figure 4-1) through the keyboard, the program continues to execute.

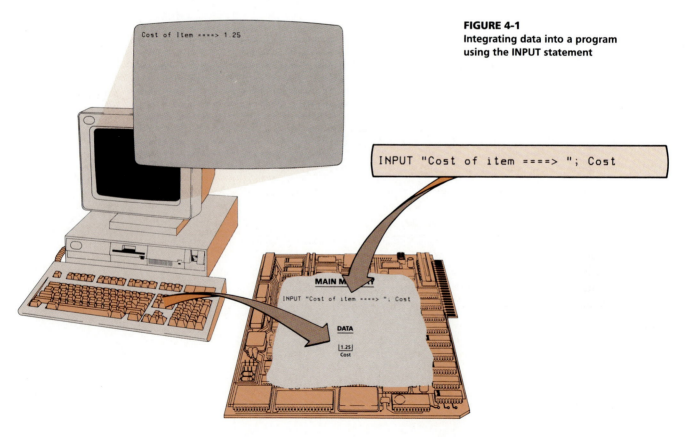

FIGURE 4-1
Integrating data into a program using the INPUT statement

The INPUT statement has two general forms, shown in Figure 4-2. With the first general form, the keyword INPUT is immediately followed by one or more variables separated by commas. When executed, this first form displays a question mark on the screen to indicate that it is waiting for the user to enter data.

The second general form of the INPUT statement shows that the programmer may enter a **prompt message** to inform the user of the required data. In this second and most often used form, the keyword INPUT is followed by the prompt message in quotation marks, a comma or semicolon after the prompt message, and a list of variables separated by commas. A semicolon after a prompt message tells the PC to display a question mark immediately after the prompt message. A comma instructs the PC not to display the question mark. Although this statement may include more than one variable, most programmers place one variable per INPUT statement.

No Prompt Message

INPUT variable, ..., variable

Prompt Message

INPUT "prompt message", variable, ..., variable

FIGURE 4-2   The general form of the INPUT statement

Figure 4-3 illustrates several examples of INPUT statements.

EXAMPLE	INPUT STATEMENT	DATA ENTERED THROUGH KEYBOARD
1	INPUT Amount, Cost	125.56, 75
2	INPUT Cus.Name$, Age, Deduction	Joe Dac, 57, 25
3	INPUT "Discount =====>", Disc	.25
4	INPUT "What is your name"; User.Name$	Marci Jean
5	PRINT "Do you want to continue?" INPUT "Enter Y for Yes, else N", Control$	Y

FIGURE 4-3   Examples of the INPUT statement

Examples 1 and 2 in Figure 4-3 show that it is not necessary to include a prompt message. When either INPUT statement is executed, a question mark displays on the screen. Examples 3 through 5 include prompt messages. In Example 3, the prompt message

```
Discount =====>
```

displays on the screen at the location of the cursor. Following the display of the prompt, the PC halts execution until the user enters the data (.25) and presses the Enter key.

In Example 4 of Figure 4-3, the following prompt displays:

```
What is your name?
```

Because we ended the prompt message with a semicolon, the PC displays the question mark after the prompt. Example 5 shows how you can utilize the PRINT statement along with the INPUT statement to display prompt messages made up of more than one line.

THE BEEP AND LOCATE STATEMENTS

wo QuickBASIC statements that are often used in tandem with the INPUT statement are the BEEP and LOCATE statements.

The BEEP Statement

When executed, the BEEP statement causes the PC's speaker to beep for a fraction of a second. Several BEEP statements in a row cause the PC to beep for a longer duration. The following line causes the PC to beep for approximately a second:

```
BEEP : BEEP : BEEP : BEEP
```

Notice the colons between the BEEP statements. In QuickBASIC, the colon allows you to place more than one statement per line. The BEEP statement is often used to alert the user that there is a problem with the program or data.

The LOCATE Statement

QuickBASIC defines the output screen as having 25 rows and 80 columns. The LOCATE statement can be used to position the cursor precisely on any one of the two thousand display positions on the screen. For example, the following line causes the PC to move the cursor to row 4, column 15:

```
LOCATE 4, 15
```

It makes no difference whether the cursor is above or below row 4 or to the right or left of column 15. The general form of the LOCATE statement is shown in Figure 4-4.

FIGURE 4-4
The general form of the LOCATE statement

```
LOCATE row, column
```

When executed, the partial program in Figure 4-5 displays the prompt message in the INPUT statement in row 6, column 12.

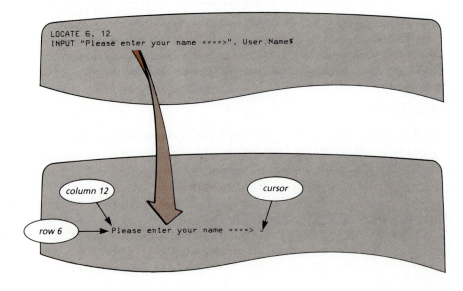

FIGURE 4-5
Use of the LOCATE statement to position the cursor

EDITING DATA ENTERED THROUGH THE KEYBOARD

*I*n most interactive applications it is required that you check the incoming data to be sure that it is reasonable. A **reasonableness check** ensures that the data is legitimate, that is, the data is within a range of acceptable values. If the data is not validated before being used, then the PC can very well generate incorrect information.

The partial program in Figure 4-6 requests that the user enter a value for the variable Item.Cost. Assume that the program specifications state that the value of Cost must be greater than zero and less than 1,000.00.

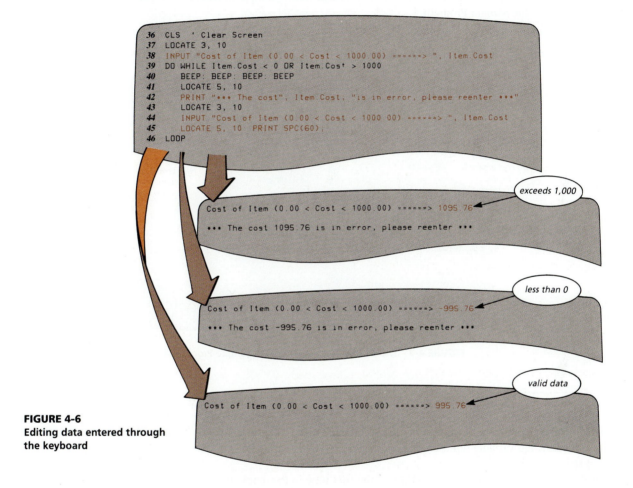

FIGURE 4-6
Editing data entered through the keyboard

When the PC executes the partial program in Figure 4-6, the CLS statement in line 36 clears the output screen. Line 37 moves the cursor to column 10 in row 3. The INPUT statement in line 38 displays the prompt message and halts execution of the program. After the user enters the value 1095.76 and presses the Enter key, the DO WHILE statement in line 39 tests the value of Item.Cost. Since it is greater than 1,000.00, control enters the loop. Line 40 causes the PC speaker to beep for a second. Due to lines 41 and 42, the PC displays an error message beginning at column 10 in row 5.

Lines 43 and 44 again cause the prompt message to display beginning at column 10 in row 3. After the user enters -995.76, the error message in row 5 is erased by the SPC function in the PRINT statement in line 45. The SPC function displays as many spaces as indicated in the parentheses. Thus, SPC(60) displays 60 spaces and in doing so erases the error message in row 5. Since -995.76 is still outside the limits, the PC reexecutes the loop and displays the error message due to line 42. Finally, when the user enters 995.76, the PC exits the loop and continues execution at the line following the LOOP statement.

Data validation is an important part of the programming process. It should be apparent that the information produced by a computer is only as accurate as the data it processes. The term **GIGO** (Garbage In—Garbage Out, pronounced GEE-GOH) is used to describe the generation of inaccurate information from the input of invalid data. Data validation should be incorporated into all programs, especially when the INPUT statement is used.

SAMPLE PROGRAM 4 — ITEM COST REPORT

*T*he sample program in this project illustrates the preparation of an item cost table that contains the cost of one to ten items. The program begins by asking the user to enter the cost of an item. The cost must be greater than zero and less than 1,000.00. After validating the entry, the sample program displays the cost table. Once the table displays, the user is asked if another table should be prepared. The user must enter a Y for yes or an N for no.

If the user enters the letter Y, the loop is executed again and the user is asked to enter the cost of the next item. If the user enters the letter N, the program displays an end-of-job message followed by termination of execution. Figure 4-7 shows the desired output results for Sample Program 4.

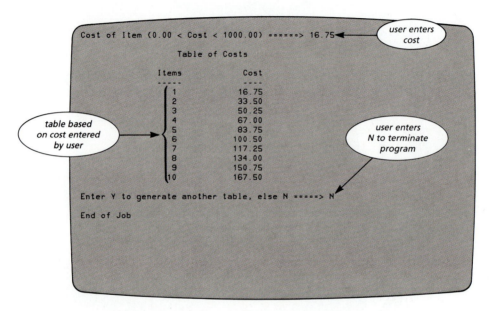

FIGURE 4-7   The desired output results for Sample Program 4

Program Flowchart

The flowchart for Sample Program 4 which produces the item cost table for one to ten items is illustrated in Figure 4-8. At the top of the flowchart, the variable representing the maximum number of items is initialized to 10 and the table format is assigned to string variables.

Control then enters the loop. Notice that this is the first time in this book that a decision symbol is not at the top of the loop. In this flowchart, the decision to terminate the loop is at the bottom. Loops that have the decision to terminate at the top are called **Do-While loops.** Loops that have the decision to terminate at the bottom are called **Do-Until loops.**

Within the major loop, the output screen is cleared and the user is requested to enter the cost of an item. Next, the cost is validated, the table headings are displayed, and a counter is initialized to one. The table is then generated by a looping process that continues while the counter is less than or equal to 10. After the table displays, the user is asked if another is desired. The decision symbol at the bottom of the Do-Until loop determines whether to continue or terminate processing on the basis of the value (Y or N) entered by the user.

Before we can code the logic shown in Figure 4-8 we need to discuss the FOR and NEXT statements.

FIGURE 4-8
The flowchart for Sample Program 4

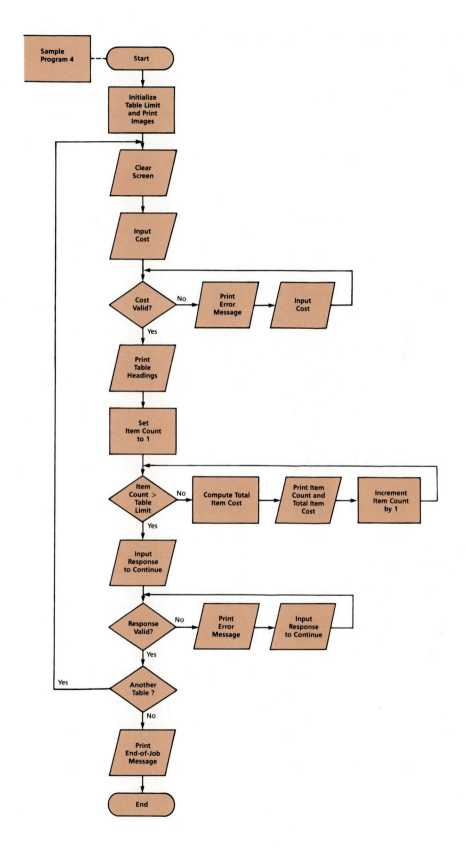

THE FOR AND NEXT STATEMENTS

*T*he FOR and NEXT statements make it possible to execute a section of a program repeatedly, with automatic changes in the value of a variable between repetitions. Whenever you have to develop a counter-controlled loop (a loop that is to be executed a specific number of times based on a counter), the FOR and NEXT statements can be used to develop it. We call such a loop a **For loop**.

Figure 4-9 illustrates how the FOR and NEXT statements can be used to implement the loop that generates the cost table described in the flowchart for Sample Program 4.

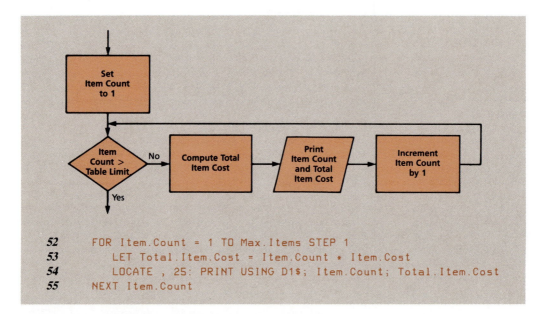

```
52      FOR Item.Count = 1 TO Max.Items STEP 1
53         LET Total.Item.Cost = Item.Count * Item.Cost
54         LOCATE , 25: PRINT USING D1$; Item.Count; Total.Item.Cost
55      NEXT Item.Count
```

FIGURE 4-9   Using the FOR and NEXT statements to implement the loop that generates the cost table

When the FOR statement in line 52 of Figure 4-9 is executed for the first time, the For loop becomes active and the variable Item.Count is set equal to one. The statements within the For loop, in this case lines 53 and 54, are executed. The NEXT statement in line 55 returns control to the FOR statement in line 52, where the value of Item.Count is incremented by the amount (1), which follows the keyword STEP. If the value of Item.Count is less than or equal to Max.Items (table limit), execution of the For loop continues. When the value of Item.Count is greater than Max.Items, control transfers to the line following NEXT Item.Count. As with other loops, notice that we indent the statements within the loop by three spaces.

The general forms of the FOR and NEXT statements are shown in Figure 4-10.

```
FOR loop-variable = initial TO limit STEP increment

   [range of statements]

NEXT loop-variable
```

FIGURE 4-10   The general forms of the FOR and NEXT statements

In Figure 4-10, the FOR statement indicates the beginning of a For loop and the NEXT statement indicates the end. The range of statements within the For loop is executed repeatedly as long as *loop-variable* is not greater than *limit*. *Loop-variable* is initially assigned the value of *initial*. Each time the range of statements is executed, *loop-variable* is increased by the value of *increment*. When *loop-variable* is greater than *limit*, control passes to the line following the corresponding NEXT statement.

If *increment* is negative, the test to terminate the For loop is reversed. The value of *loop-variable* is decremented each time through the For loop, and the For loop is executed while *loop-variable* is greater than or equal to *limit*. If the keyword STEP is not included in a FOR statement, then the increment value is automatically set to one.

Figure 4-11 illustrates several valid FOR statements.

EXAMPLE	FOR STATEMENT
1	FOR Count = 1 TO 100 STEP 1
2	FOR X = 5 TO Y STEP 3
3	FOR Amount = 1.25 TO 7.35 STEP .05
4	FOR Tax = A TO B STEP C
5	FOR S = 0 TO -35 STEP -3
6	FOR X = 1 TO 10

FIGURE 4-11   Examples of valid FOR statements

In Example 1 of Figure 4-11, the For loop is executed 100 times. Example 2 points out that the initial and increment values can be values other than one. Example 3 initializes Amount to 1.25 for the first pass. Thereafter, the value .05 is added to Amount each time the range of statements is executed. Hence, Amount takes on the values 1.25, 1.30, 1.35, 1.40, and so on, until Amount exceeds 7.35.

Example 4 shows that the initial, limit, and increment values can be variables. Example 5 includes a negative increment (–3). Thus, the test is reversed and S must be less than –35 before the For loop terminates. Finally, Example 6 illustrates a FOR statement without the keyword STEP. In this case, the increment value is automatically set to one.

The QuickBASIC Program

The program in Figure 4-12 corresponds to the program flowchart in Figure 4-8.

FIGURE 4-12
Sample Program 4

```
1  ' ********************************************************************
2  ' *  Sample Program 4                         September 15, 1994  *
3  ' *  Item Cost Report                                             *
4  ' *  J. S. Quasney                                                *
5  ' *                                                               *
6  ' *  This program displays a table of costs of 1 to 10 items.    *
7  ' *  The user enters the cost per item and the program           *
8  ' *  displays the table of costs.                                *
9  ' *       The cost per item entered by the user is validated     *
10 ' *  (greater than zero and less than 1000.00).  After the       *
11 ' *  table is displayed the user is asked if another table       *
12 ' *  should be generated.                                        *
13 ' *       This activity continues until the user indicates       *
14 ' *  that no more tables are to be generated.                    *
15 ' *                                                               *
16 ' *  Variables:  Item.Cost        -- Cost of item                *
17 ' *              Item.Count       -- Item count                  *
18 ' *              Max.Items        -- Maximum number of items     *
19 ' *                                   in table                   *
20 ' *              Total.Item.Cost  -- Cost of items               *
21 ' *              Control$         -- Response to continue        *
22 ' *              H1$, H2$, H3$, D1$, T1$ -- Print images         *
23 ' ********************************************************************
24
```

(continued)

FIGURE 4-12
(continued)

```
25  ' ******************** Initialization ********************
26  LET Max.Items = 10
27  LET H1$ = "    Table of Costs"
28  LET H2$ = "Items            Cost"
29  LET H3$ = "-----          ----"
30  LET D1$ = "  ##         ##,###.##"
31  LET T1$ = "End of Job"
32
33  ' ****************** Generate Cost Table ********************
34  DO
35     ' *********** Accept and Validate Cost of Item ***********
36     CLS  ' Clear Screen
37     LOCATE 3, 10
38     INPUT "Cost of Item (0.00 < Cost < 1000.00) ======> ", Item.Cost
39     DO WHILE Item.Cost < 0 OR Item.Cost > 1000
40        BEEP: BEEP: BEEP: BEEP
41        LOCATE 5, 10
42        PRINT "*** The cost"; Item.Cost; "is in error, please reenter ***"
43        LOCATE 3, 10
44        INPUT "Cost of Item (0.00 < Cost < 1000.00) ======> ", Item.Cost
45        LOCATE 5, 10: PRINT SPC(60);
46     LOOP
47
48     ' *************** Generate Table of Costs ***************
49     LOCATE 5, 25: PRINT H1$
50     LOCATE 7, 25: PRINT H2$
51     LOCATE 8, 25: PRINT H3$
52     FOR Item.Count = 1 TO Max.Items STEP 1
53        LET Total.Item.Cost = Item.Count * Item.Cost
54        LOCATE , 25: PRINT USING D1$; Item.Count; Total.Item.Cost
55     NEXT Item.Count
56
57     ' ******** Accept and Validate Response to Continue ********
58     LOCATE 20, 10
59     INPUT "Enter Y to generate another table, else N =====> ", Control$
60     DO WHILE Control$ <> "N" AND Control$ <> "Y"
61        BEEP: BEEP: BEEP: BEEP
62        LOCATE 22, 10
63        PRINT "*** Response in error, please reenter ***"
64        LOCATE 20, 10
65        INPUT "Enter Y to generate another table, else N =====> ", Control$
66        LOCATE 22, 10: PRINT SPC(50);
67     LOOP
68
69  LOOP UNTIL Control$ = "N"
70
71  ' ********************** Wrap-Up **************************
72  LOCATE 22, 10
73  PRINT T1$
74  END
```

Discussion of Sample Program 4

When Sample Program 4 is executed, the variables in lines 26 through 31 are initialized. Line 26 initializes Max.Items (table limit) to 10. Lines 27 through 31 define the table format. The variables are used later in the PRINT statements in lines 49 through 51, 54, and 73.

The DO statement in line 34 indicates the beginning of a Do-Until loop. With a Do-Until loop, the condition that determines whether the loop should continue is in the LOOP statement (line 69). As shown in Figure 4-13, there are two basic types of loops. The Do-While loop has the decision symbol at the top of the loop. The Do-Until loop has the decision symbol at the bottom of the loop. If the decision is at the top (Figure 4-13A), use the DO WHILE and LOOP statements. If the decision is at the bottom (Figure 4-13B), use the DO and LOOP UNTIL statements.

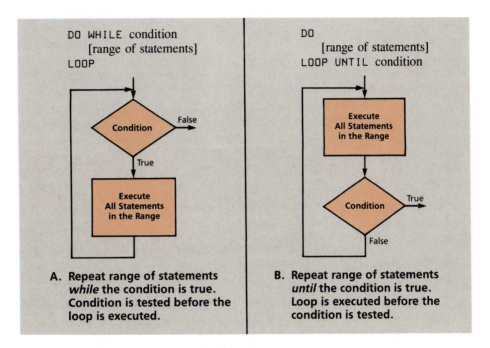

FIGURE 4-13   The two basic types of loops and the statements in QuickBASIC which should be used to implement them

Upon entering the Do-Until loop, the screen is cleared by line 36. Lines 37 through 46 accept and validate the cost of the item entered by the user. Lines 49 through 51 display the table title and column headings. Lines 52 through 55 compute and display the rows of the table. Notice in line 54 that the LOCATE statement does not include a row number. When the LOCATE statement is written in this fashion, it references the current row, which is one greater than the one referenced by the previously executed PRINT or PRINT USING statement. Hence, each time line 54 is executed in the For loop, the PRINT USING statement begins printing in column 25 of the next row. Notice in lines 49 through 51 and 54 that it is common practice to incorporate both the LOCATE and PRINT statements on the same line. Of course, it is important that you separate the two statements with the colon.

After the table is displayed on the screen, lines 58 through 67 accept and validate a response from the user that indicates whether the Do-Until loop should continue. In this case, only two values, Y and N, are acceptable (line 60). If the user enters a Y, line 69 causes the PC to continue execution at the top of the loop (line 34). If the user enters the value N, the condition in line 69 is false. Thus, control passes to line 72 and an end-of-job message is displayed followed by termination of execution of the program.

Figure 4-14 shows the display of Sample Program 4 when the value 579.46 is entered as the cost of an item.

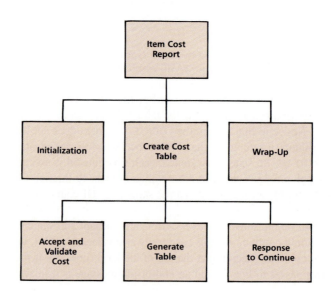

```
Cost of Item (0.00 < Cost < 1000.00) =======> 579.46

                    Table of Costs

            Items             Cost
            -----             ----
              1              579.46
              2            1,158.92
              3            1,738.38
              4            2,317.84
              5            2,897.30
              6            3,476.76
              7            4,056.22
              8            4,635.68
              9            5,215.14
             10            5,794.60

Enter Y to generate another table, else N =====> N

End of Job
```

FIGURE 4-14
The results displayed due to the
execution of Sample Program 4
and a cost per item of $579.46

AN INTRODUCTION TO THE TOP-DOWN APPROACH

op-down programming is a divide and conquer strategy used by programmers to solve large problems. The first step in top-down programming is to divide the task into smaller, more manageable subtasks through the use of a top-down chart. Figure 4-15 illustrates a top-down chart for the problem solved by Sample Program 4.

FIGURE 4-15
A top-down chart for the problem solved by Sample Program 4

A top-down chart differs from a program flowchart in that it does not show decision-making logic or flow of control. A program flowchart shows *how* to solve the problem. A top-down chart shows *what* has to be done.

A top-down chart is very similar to a company's organization chart where each lower level subtask carries out a function for its superior task. In Figure 4-15, the top box (Item Cost Report) represents the complete task. The next level of boxes (Initialization, Create Cost Table, and Wrap-Up) shows the subtasks that are required to solve the task of the top box. The lowest level of boxes (Accept and Validate Cost Item, Generate Table, and Response to Continue) indicates the subtasks required to create a table. Usually, a task is divided into lower level subtasks whenever it appears to be too complicated or lengthy to stand by itself.

Implementing the Top-Down Approach

Once the larger, more complex problem has been decomposed into smaller pieces, a solution to each subtask can be designed and coded. We call the group of statements that are associated with a single programming task a **subroutine**, or **module**.

The subroutines that formulate a program solution begin with a name, followed immediately by a colon (:), and end with a RETURN statement. Subroutines are *called* by their superior modules using the GOSUB statement. When a subroutine has completed its task, control returns to the superior module via a RETURN statement. The rules regarding a subroutine name are the same as for a variable name.

THE GOSUB AND RETURN STATEMENTS

he GOSUB statement is used to call a subroutine. As shown in Figure 4-16, the keyword GOSUB is immediately followed by the subroutine name to which control is transferred. Once control transfers, the instructions in the subroutine are executed.

FIGURE 4-16
The general form of the GOSUB statement

    GOSUB subroutine-name

The RETURN statement (Figure 4-17) at the bottom of the subroutine returns control to the statement following the corresponding GOSUB in the superior module.

FIGURE 4-17
The general form of the RETURN statement

    RETURN

Consider the partial program on the next page in Figure 4-18 and the following important points regarding the implementation of the top-down approach:

- The END statement is the last statement in the Main module. Control returns to DOS through this statement.
- Indent by three spaces the statements within modules.
- So that lower level modules can easily be located, they should be placed below their superior module and in the order in which they are called.

FIGURE 4-18
Implementing the top-down
chart in Figure 4-15

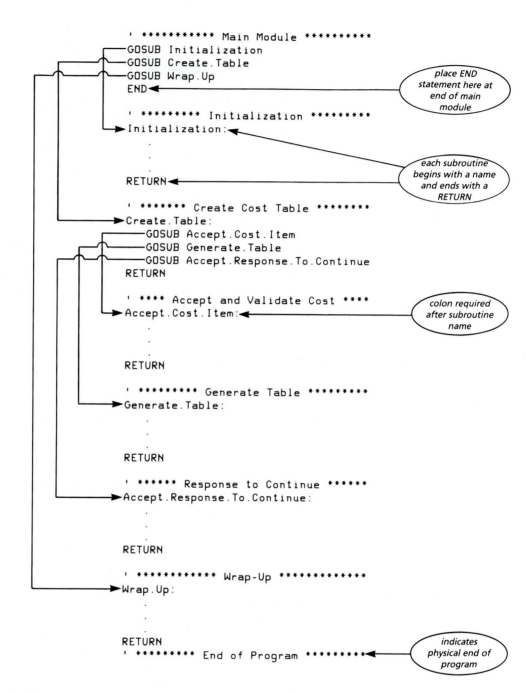

```
' ********** Main Module **********
GOSUB Initialization
GOSUB Create.Table
GOSUB Wrap.Up
END

' ******** Initialization ********
Initialization:
    .
    .
    .
RETURN

' ******* Create Cost Table ********
Create.Table:
    GOSUB Accept.Cost.Item
    GOSUB Generate.Table
    GOSUB Accept.Response.To.Continue
RETURN

' **** Accept and Validate Cost ****
Accept.Cost.Item:
    .
    .
    .
RETURN

' ******** Generate Table ********
Generate.Table:
    .
    .
    .
RETURN

' ****** Response to Continue ******
Accept.Response.To.Continue:
    .
    .
    .
RETURN

' ************ Wrap-Up ************
Wrap.Up:
    .
    .
    .
RETURN
' ********* End of Program *********
```

place END statement here at end of main module

each subroutine begins with a name and ends with a RETURN

colon required after subroutine name

indicates physical end of program

A modified version of Sample Program 4 which utilizes the top-down approach is shown in Figure 4-19. The coding corresponds to the top-down chart in Figure 4-15.

FIGURE 4-19
A top-down version of Sample Program 4

```
1    ' ********************************************************
2    ' *   Sample Program 4 Modified          September 15, 1994  *
3    ' *   Item Cost Report                                       *
4    ' *   J. S. Quasney                                          *
5    ' *                                                          *
6    ' *   This program displays a table of costs of 1 to 10 items. *
7    ' *   The user enters the cost per item and the program     *
8    ' *   displays the table of costs.                          *
9    ' *        The cost per item entered by the user is validated *
10   ' *   (greater than zero and less than 1000.00).  After the *
11   ' *   table is displayed the user is asked if another table *
12   ' *   should be generated.                                  *
13   ' *        This activity continues until the user indicates *
14   ' *   that no more tables are to be generated.              *
15   ' *                                                          *
16   ' *   Variables:  Item.Cost       -- Cost of item           *
17   ' *               Item.Count      -- Item count             *
18   ' *               Max.Items       -- Maximum number of items *
19   ' *                                   in table              *
20   ' *               Total.Item.Cost -- Cost of items          *
21   ' *               Control$        -- Response to continue   *
22   ' *               H1$, H2$, H3$, D1$, T1$ -- Print images   *
23   ' ********************************************************
24
25   ' ********************************************************
26   ' *                    Main Module                          *
27   ' ********************************************************
28   GOSUB Initialization
29   GOSUB Create.Table
30   GOSUB Wrap.Up
31   END
32
33   ' ********************************************************
34   ' *                    Initialization                       *
35   ' ********************************************************
36   Initialization:
37      LET Max.Items = 10
38      LET H1$ = "    Table of Costs"
39      LET H2$ = "Items            Cost"
40      LET H3$ = "-----            ----"
41      LET D1$ = "  ##          ##,###.##"
42      LET T1$ = "End of Job"
43   RETURN
44
45   ' ********************************************************
46   ' *                    Create Cost Table                    *
47   ' ********************************************************
48   Create.Table:
49      DO
50         GOSUB Accept.Cost.Item
51         GOSUB Generate.Table
52         GOSUB Accept.Response.To.Continue
53      LOOP UNTIL Control$ = "N"
54   RETURN
55
```

(continued)

FIGURE 4-19
(continued)

```
56  ' ******************************************************************
57  ' *              Accept and Validate Cost of Item                 *
58  ' ******************************************************************
59  Accept.Cost.Item:
60     CLS   ' Clear Screen
61     LOCATE 3, 10
62     INPUT "Cost of Item (0.00 < Cost < 1000.00) ======> ", Item.Cost
63     DO WHILE Item.Cost < 0 OR Item.Cost > 1000
64        BEEP: BEEP: BEEP: BEEP
65        LOCATE 5, 10
66        PRINT "*** The cost"; Item.Cost; "is in error, please reenter ***"
67        LOCATE 3, 10
68        INPUT "Cost of Item (0.00 < Cost < 1000.00) ======> ", Item.Cost
69        LOCATE 5, 10: PRINT SPC(60);
70     LOOP
71  RETURN
72
73  ' ******************************************************************
74  ' *                   Generate Table of Costs                     *
75  ' ******************************************************************
76  Generate.Table:
77     LOCATE 5, 25: PRINT H1$
78     LOCATE 7, 25: PRINT H2$
79     LOCATE 8, 25: PRINT H3$
80     FOR Item.Count = 1 TO Max.Items STEP 1
81        LET Total.Item.Cost = Item.Count * Item.Cost
82        LOCATE , 25: PRINT USING D1$; Item.Count; Total.Item.Cost
83     NEXT Item.Count
84  RETURN
85
86  ' ******************************************************************
87  ' *            Accept and Validate Response to Continue           *
88  ' ******************************************************************
89  Accept.Response.To.Continue:
90     LOCATE 20, 10
91     INPUT "Enter Y to generate another table, else N =====> ", Control$
92     DO WHILE Control$ <> "N" AND Control$ <> "Y"
93        BEEP: BEEP: BEEP: BEEP
94        LOCATE 22, 10
95        PRINT "*** Response in error, please reenter ***"
96        LOCATE 20, 10
97        INPUT "Enter Y to generate another table, else N =====> ", Control$
98        LOCATE 22, 10: PRINT SPC(50);
99     LOOP
100 RETURN
101
102 ' ******************************************************************
103 ' *                          Wrap-Up                              *
104 ' ******************************************************************
105 Wrap.Up:
106    LOCATE 22, 10
107    PRINT T1$
108 RETURN
109 ' ******************* End of Program **********************
```

Discussion of Sample Program 4 Modified

When the modified version of Sample Program 4 in Figure 4-19 executes, line 28 in the Main module transfers control to the Initialization module which begins at line 36. After lines 37 through 42 are executed, the RETURN statement in line 43 transfers control back to line 29 in the Main module. Next, line 29 transfers control to the Create.Table module (lines 48 through 54). In this module, the Do-Until loop includes three GOSUB statements. Each time through this loop, a cost table such as the one in Figure 4-20 is generated.

When the user enters the letter N in response to the INPUT statement in line 97, control passes back to line 53. Since the condition in line 53 is true, control passes to the RETURN statement in line 54. Line 54 returns control to line 30. Next, line 30 transfers control to the Wrap.Up module which begins at line 105. After the end-of-job message is displayed, control returns to line 31 in the Main module and the program terminates execution.

```
Cost of Item (0.00 < Cost < 1000.00) ======> 67.50

                   Table of Costs

              Items              Cost
              -----              ----
                1               67.50
                2              135.00
                3              202.50
                4              270.00
                5              337.50
                6              405.00
                7              472.50
                8              540.00
                9              607.50
               10              675.00

Enter Y to generate another table, else N =====> N

End of Job
```

FIGURE 4-20   The results displayed due to the execution of the modified Sample Program 4 and a cost per item of $67.50

TRY IT YOURSELF EXERCISES

1. What is displayed if each of the following programs are executed?
   a. X is assigned the value 2, and Y is assigned the value 4.

```
' Exercise 1.a
INPUT "Enter values for X and Y ===> ", X, Y
Sum = X + Y
Diff = Y - X
Prod = X * Y
Quot = X / Y
PRINT Sum, Diff
PRINT Prod, Quot
END
```

b.

```
' Exercise 1.b
Total = 0
GOSUB Increment.Total
PRINT Total
GOSUB Increment.Total
PRINT Total
GOSUB Increment.Total
PRINT Total
Total = Total - 6
PRINT Total
END
' Increment Total
Increment.Total:
   Total = Total + 2
RETURN
```

c. Selling.Price and Discount.Rate are assigned $30.00 and 25%, respectively.

```
' Exercise 1.c
' *********************************
' *           Main Module         *
' *********************************
GOSUB Accept.Data
GOSUB Compute.Discount
GOSUB Display.Discount
END


' *********************************
' *       Accept Operator Data    *
' *********************************
Accept.Data:
   CLS  ' Clear Screen
   INPUT "Selling Price ===>", Selling.Price
   INPUT "Discount Rate in % ===>", Discount.Rate
RETURN


' *********************************
' *          Compute Discount     *
' *********************************
Compute.Discount:
   Discount.Rate = Discount.Rate / 100
   Discount = Discount.Rate * Selling.Price
RETURN


' *********************************
' *           Discount Amount     *
' *********************************
Display.Discount:
   PRINT "Discount ======>"; Discount
RETURN

' *********** End of Program *******
```

2. Is the following partial program invalid? If it is invalid, indicate why.

```
' Exercise 2
' Main Module
    .
    .
    .
GOSUB Calculate
' Calculate Square
Calculate:
    X = X * X
RETURN
END
```

3. Write a sequence of LOCATE and PRINT statements that will display the word Retail beginning in column 12 of row 15.

4. Write a series of statements that will display the number 22 in column 22 of row 22.

5. Consider the two following types of loops:

a. DO WHILE ... LOOP

b. DO ... LOOP UNTIL

Answer the following questions for each type of loop:

(1) Does the loop terminate when the condition is true or false?

(2) What is the minimum number of times the range of statements in the loop is executed?

(3) Is the test to terminate the loop made before or after the range of statements is executed?

6. At what column and row is the cursor after the following two statements are executed?

```
LOCATE 15, 34
LOCATE 17
```

7. Identify the syntax and logic error(s), if any, in each of the following:

a. FOR X = 1 TO 6 STEP -1

b. FOR Amt = 1 TO Sq

c. FOR T$ = 0 TO 7

d. FOR Value = 10 TO 1

e. FOR H = A TO B STEP -B

8. How many times does the PRINT statement execute when the following program is executed?

```
' Exercise 8
FOR J = 1 TO 30
    FOR N = 1 TO 20
        FOR I = 1 TO 3
            PRINT J, N, I
        NEXT I
    NEXT N
NEXT J
END
```

9. Explain the purpose of the following statement. What are the colons used for?

```
BEEP : BEEP : BEEP : BEEP
```

STUDENT ASSIGNMENTS

STUDENT ASSIGNMENT 1: Weekly Pay Rate Table

Instructions: Design and code a top-down QuickBASIC program, such as the one in Figure 4-19, to generate the weekly pay rate table shown under OUTPUT. Request that the user enter through the keyboard an hourly rate between $3.35 and $30.00, inclusive. Validate the entry. Use a For loop to generate a table of 10 hourly rates in increments of $0.50 and the corresponding weekly rates. A weekly rate is equal to 40 times the hourly rate. After the table displays, request the user to enter the letter Y to generate another table or the letter N to terminate the program. Use the following top-down chart as a guide to solving this problem:

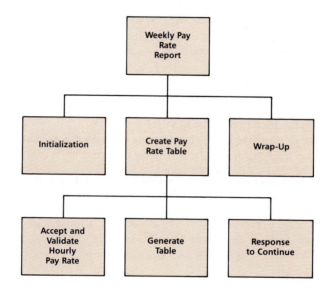

INPUT: Use the following sample data:

Table 1 – Hourly rate $6.75
Table 2 – Hourly rate $22.50

OUTPUT: The following results are displayed for the first table:

```
Initial Pay Rate (3.35 <= Cost <= 30.00) ======> 6.75

     Table of Hourly and Weekly Rates

       Hourly                Weekly
       Rate                  Rate
       ------                ------
        6.75                 270.00
        7.25                 290.00
        7.75                 310.00
        8.25                 330.00
        8.75                 350.00
        9.25                 370.00
        9.75                 390.00
       10.25                 410.00
       10.75                 430.00
       11.25                 450.00

Enter Y to generate another table, else N =====> Y
```

STUDENT ASSIGNMENT 2: Metric Conversion Table

Instructions: Design and code a top-down QuickBASIC program, such as the one in Figure 4-19, to generate a metric conversion table as shown on the next page in the printout. Request that the user enter through the keyboard an initial metric value, a limit metric value, and an increment metric value. Validate each entry. The initial metric value must be between 1 and 1,500, inclusive. The limit metric value must be greater than the initial metric value and less than 2,000. The increment metric value must be greater than zero and less than or equal to 100.

Use a For loop to generate a table of the metric values between the initial metric value and limit metric value. For each metric value, print the equivalent yards, feet, and inches. There are 39.37 inches in a meter, 12 inches in a foot, and 3 feet in a yard. After the table prints, request the user to enter the letter Y to generate another table or the letter N to terminate the program. Use the following top-down chart as a guide to solving this problem:

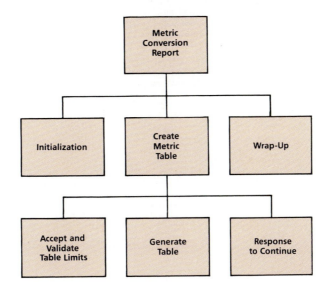

Before you print each table, use the following statement to move the paper in the printer to the top of the next page:

```
LPRINT CHR$(12);
```

This LPRINT statement prints the value of the function CHR$(12), which is the form feed character.

INPUT: Use the following sample data:

Table 1 – Initial meters 100, Limit meters 200, Increment meters 10
Table 2 – Initial meters 140, Limit meters 160, Increment meters 2

OUTPUT: The following results display on the screen for the Table 1 data:

```
Initial Meter Value (1 <= Initial Meter <= 1500) ==> 100

Limit Meter Value (Initial Meter < Limit Meter < 2,000) ======> 200

Increment Meter Value (0 < Increment Meter <= 100) ======> 10

********* Report Being Printed On Printer *********

Enter Y to generate another table, else N =====> Y
```

Student Assignment 2 (continued)

The following results are printed on the printer for the Table 1 data:

```
            Metric Conversion Table

    Meters      Yards      Feet      Inches
    ------      -----      ----      ------
    100.00     109.36    328.08     3,937.00
    110.00     120.30    360.89     4,330.70
    120.00     131.23    393.70     4,724.40
    130.00     142.17    426.51     5,118.10
    140.00     153.11    459.32     5,511.80
    150.00     164.04    492.13     5,905.50
    160.00     174.98    524.93     6,299.20
    170.00     185.91    557.74     6,692.90
    180.00     196.85    590.55     7,086.60
    190.00     207.79    623.36     7,480.30
    200.00     218.72    656.17     7,874.00

    End of Table
```

PROJECT 5

Sequential File Processing

*I*n the first four projects we emphasized the importance of integrating data into the program. You learned that data may be entered into a program through the use of the INPUT statement or the READ and DATA statements. This project presents a third method for entering data—the use of data files. With data files, the data is stored in auxiliary storage rather than in the program itself. This technique is used primarily for dealing with large amounts of data.

QuickBASIC includes a set of file-handling statements that allow a user to do the following:

- Open a file
- Read data from a file
- Write data to a file
- Test for the end-of-file
- Close a file

FILE ORGANIZATION

*Q*uickBASIC provides for two types of file organization: sequential and random. A file that is organized sequentially is called a **sequential file** and is limited to sequential processing. This means that the records can be processed only in the order in which they are placed in the file. Conceptually, a sequential file is identical to the use of DATA statements within a QuickBASIC program.

The second type of file organization, **random files**, allows you to process the records in the file in any order. If the fifth record is required and it is stored in a random file, then the program may access it without reading the first four records. Random files are not discussed in this project.

CREATING A SEQUENTIAL DATA FILE

*T*his section presents the OPEN, WRITE #n, and CLOSE statements. These statements are used to create a sequential data file. The OPEN statement is used to activate the file. The WRITE #n statement is used to write a record to the file. And the CLOSE statement is used to deactivate the file.

Opening Sequential Files

Before any file can be read from or written to, it must be opened by the OPEN statement. The OPEN statement identifies by name the file to be processed. It indicates whether the file is to be read from or written to. It also assigns the file a filenumber that can be used by statements that need to reference the file in question.

The general form of the OPEN statement is shown in Figure 5-1.

FIGURE 5-1
The general form of the OPEN statement

> OPEN filespec FOR mode AS #filenumber
>
> where **filespec** is the name of the file;
> **mode** is one of the following:
> APPEND opens file so that records can be added to the end of the file;
> INPUT opens file to read beginning with the first record;
> OUTPUT opens file to write records; and
> **filenumber** is a numeric expression whose value is between 1 and 255.

As described in Figure 5-1, a sequential data file may be opened for input, output, or append. If a file is opened for input, the program can only read records from it. If a file is opened for output, the program can only write records to it. The Append mode allows you to write records to the end of a file that already has records in it. Figure 5-2 illustrates several OPEN statements.

EXAMPLE	STATEMENT
1	OPEN "B:PAYROLL.DAT" FOR OUTPUT AS #4
2	OPEN "ACCOUNT.DAT" FOR APPEND AS #2
3	OPEN Filename$ FOR OUTPUT AS #1
4	OPEN "PART.DAT" FOR INPUT AS #1

FIGURE 5-2
Examples of OPEN statements

The OPEN statement in Example 1 in Figure 5-2 opens PAYROLL.DAT on the B drive for output as filenumber 4. Since it is opened for output, you can only write records to PAYROLL.DAT. If you attempt to read a record, the PC will display a diagnostic message.

Example 2 opens the data file ACCOUNT.DAT for append as filenumber 2. Records can only be written to a data file opened for append. If ACCOUNT.DAT exists, records are written in sequence after the last record. If ACCOUNT.DAT does not exist, the PC creates it and the data file is treated as if it were open for output.

Example 3 in Figure 5-2 shows that in an OPEN statement you can use a string variable as the data file name. The assumption is that you will assign a file name to the string variable before the OPEN statement is executed.

Example 4 opens the data file PART.DAT on the default drive for input as filenumber 1. A file opened for input means we plan to read data from it. Later in this project we will show how data can be read from a data file.

Closing Sequential Files

When a program is finished reading or writing to a file, it must close the file with the CLOSE statement. The CLOSE statement terminates the association between the file and the filenumber assigned in the OPEN statement. If a file is being written to, the CLOSE statement ensures that the last record is written to the data file.

The general form of the CLOSE statement is shown in Figure 5-3.

FIGURE 5-3
The general form of the CLOSE statement

```
CLOSE

or

CLOSE #filenumber₁, ..., #filenumberₙ
```

The CLOSE statement terminates access to a data file. For example, CLOSE #1 causes the data file assigned to filenumber 1 to be closed. Any other files previously opened by the program remain open. Following the close of a specified file, the filenumber may be assigned again to the same file or to a different file by an OPEN statement. The keyword CLOSE without any filenumber, closes all opened data files.

Note that when executed, the END statement closes all opened files before terminating execution of the program.

Writing Data to a Sequential File

To write data to a sequential file, we use the WRITE #n statement. The WRITE #n statement writes data in a format required by the INPUT #n statement. The format requirement is similar to that of the READ and DATA statements—all data items are separated by commas. The WRITE #n statement even goes one step further by surrounding all string data items written to the file with quotation marks.

The general form of the WRITE #n statement is shown in Figure 5-4.

FIGURE 5-4
The general form of the
WRITE #n statement

```
WRITE #filenumber, variable₁, variable₂, ..., variableₙ
```

Consider the WRITE #n statement in Figure 5-5. Assume that Part.No$ = 129, Description$ = Hex Bolt, On.Hand = 200, and Wholesale = 1.26. The WRITE #n statement transmits the record shown to the sequential file assigned to filenumber 1. The WRITE #n statement causes a comma to be placed between the data items in the record. Quotation marks are placed around the values of the string variables Part.No$ and Description$, and a carriage return character ↵ is appended to the last data item written to form the record.

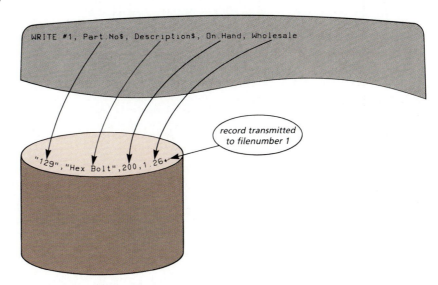

FIGURE 5-5
Writing data to a data file

SAMPLE PROGRAM 5A — CREATING A SEQUENTIAL DATA FILE

*I*n this sample program, we create a sequential data file (PART.DAT) on the B drive from the part data shown in Figure 5-6. The data must be written in a format that is consistent with the INPUT #n statement. We use a series of LOCATE, PRINT, and INPUT statements to display the screen on the screen layout form shown on the next page in Figure 5-7. As part of the Wrap-Up module, the number of records written to PART.DAT is displayed.

PART NUMBER	DESCRIPTION	ON HAND	WHOLESALE PRICE
323	Canon PC-25	12	$799.92
432	Timex Watch	53	27.95
567	12 Inch Monitor	34	50.30
578	Epson Printer	23	179.95
745	6 Inch Frying Pan	17	9.71
812	Mr. Coffee	39	21.90
923	4-Piece Toaster	7	17.57

FIGURE 5-6   The data to be written to the sequential file PART.DAT

Notice that we are not validating the data entered through the keyboard in this sample program so that we can present a clear-cut example of how to create a sequential file. In a production environment, reasonableness checks are always considered for the part number, description, on hand, and wholesale price. Data should always be validated before it is written to a file.

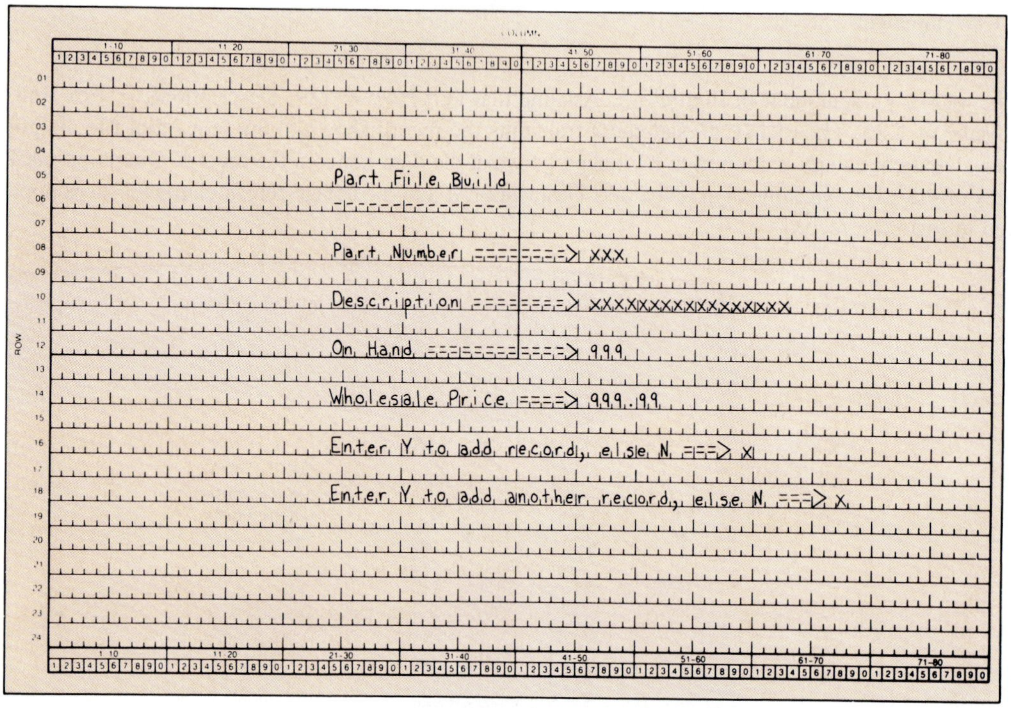

FIGURE 5-7   A screen layout form for Sample Program 5A

A top-down chart, a program flowchart for each module, a program solution, and a discussion of the program solution follow.

Top-Down Chart and Program Flowcharts

Figure 5-8 illustrates the top-down chart and corresponding program flowcharts for each module in Sample Program 5A. In the Initialization module, the record counter is initialized to zero and the data file PART.DAT is opened. The Do-Until loop in the Build File module executes until the user indicates that there are no more records to enter. Within the Do-Until loop, a part record is accepted through the keyboard. After each record is entered, the user must enter the letter Y to add the record. This entry gives the user the opportunity to cancel the record while it is displayed on the screen, but before it is added to PART.DAT. After all the records are entered, the Wrap-Up module displays the number of records written to PART.DAT.

In the program flowcharts, notice that the OPEN, WRITE #n, and CLOSE statements are represented by the Input/Output symbol (parallelogram).

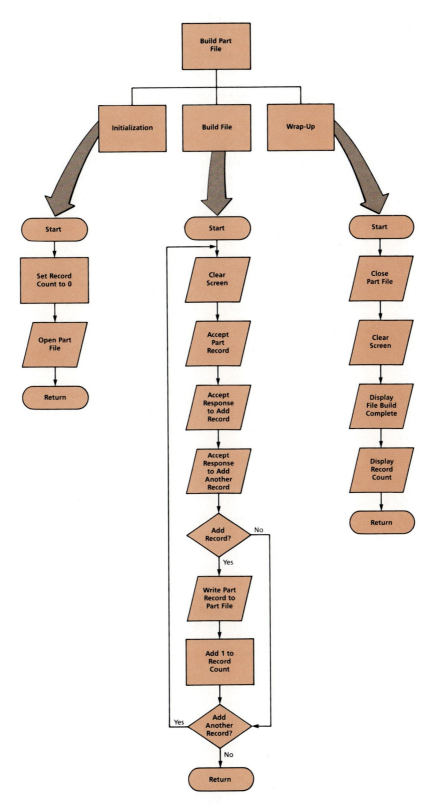

FIGURE 5-8   A top-down chart and corresponding program flowc for Sample Program 5A

The QuickBASIC Program

The program in Figure 5-9 corresponds to the top-down chart and program flowcharts in Figure 5-8.

FIGURE 5-9
Sample Program 5A

```
 1   ' **************************************************************
 2   ' *  Sample Program 5A                     September 15, 1994  *
 3   ' *  Build Part File                                           *
 4   ' *  J. S. Quasney                                             *
 5   ' *                                                            *
 6   ' *  This program builds the data file PART.DAT.               *
 7   ' *  The user enters each part record through the keyboard.    *
 8   ' *  After the record is entered, it is written to PART.DAT.   *
 9   ' *      The number of records written to PART.DAT is          *
10   ' *  displayed as part of the Wrap-Up module.                  *
11   ' *                                                            *
12   ' *  Variables:  Part.No$        -- Part number                *
13   ' *              Description$    -- Part description           *
14   ' *              On.Hand         -- Number on hand             *
15   ' *              Wholesale       -- Wholesale price of part    *
16   ' *              Record.Count    -- Count of records added to  *
17   ' *                                 PART.DAT                    *
18   ' *              Add.Rec$        -- Indicates if record is to  *
19   ' *                                 be written to PART.DAT     *
20   ' *              Control$        -- Controls Do-Until loop     *
21   ' **************************************************************
22
23   ' **************************************************************
24   ' *                      Main Module                           *
25   ' **************************************************************
26   GOSUB Initialization
27   GOSUB Build.File
28   GOSUB Wrap.Up
29   END
30
31   ' **************************************************************
32   ' *                     Initialization                         *
33   ' **************************************************************
34   Initialization:
35      Record.Count = 0
36      OPEN "B:PART.DAT" FOR OUTPUT AS #1
37   RETURN
38
```

FIGURE 5-9
(continued)

```
39  ' *******************************************************************
40  ' *                          Build File                             *
41  ' *******************************************************************
42  Build.File:
43     DO
44        CLS   ' Clear Screen
45        LOCATE 5, 25: PRINT "Part File Build"
46        LOCATE 6, 25: PRINT "---------------"
47        LOCATE 8, 25: INPUT "Part Number =======> ", Part.No$
48        LOCATE 10, 25: INPUT "Description =======> ", Description$
49        LOCATE 12, 25: INPUT "On Hand ===========> ", On.Hand
50        LOCATE 14, 25: INPUT "Wholesale Price ===> ", Wholesale
51        LOCATE 16, 25: INPUT "Enter Y to add record, else N ===> ", Add.Rec$
52        LOCATE 18, 25
53        INPUT "Enter Y to add another record, else N ===> ", Control$
54        IF Add.Rec$ = "Y" OR Add.Rec$ = "y" THEN
55           WRITE #1, Part.No$, Description$, On.Hand, Wholesale
56           Record.Count = Record.Count + 1
57        END IF
58     LOOP UNTIL Control$ = "N" OR Control$ = "n"
59  RETURN
60
61  ' *******************************************************************
62  ' *                           Wrap-Up                               *
63  ' *******************************************************************
64  Wrap.Up:
65     CLOSE #1
66     CLS   ' Clear Screen
67     LOCATE 10, 15: PRINT "Creation of PART.DAT is Complete"
68     LOCATE 14, 15
69     PRINT "Total Number of Records in PART.DAT ===>"; Record.Count
70  RETURN
71
72  ' ******************** End of Program ********************
```

Discussion of the Program Solution

When Sample Program 5A is executed, line 36 of the Initialization module opens PART.DAT for output on the B drive as filenumber 1. In the Build File module, lines 45 through 53 of the Do-Until loop accepts data values through the keyboard. The display due to the execution of these lines for the first record entered by the operator is shown on the next page in Figure 5-10. Notice the two messages at the bottom of the screen. The first message (displayed due to line 51) gives the operator the opportunity to reject the transaction by assigning Add.Rec$ a value other than Y (or y). The second message (displayed due to line 53) requests that the operator enter a Y (or y) to add another record to the part file.

Owing to line 54, the part record is added by the WRITE #n statement if Add.Rec$ is equal to Y (or y). Line 58 controls the Do-Until loop. If Control$ equals N (or n), then the loop terminates, and control returns to line 28 of the Main module. If Control$ is equal to any other value, then the loop continues.

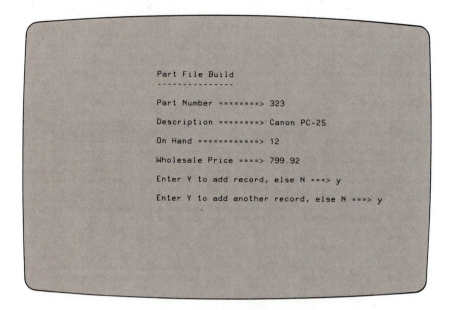

FIGURE 5-10
The display after the first part record is entered due to the execution of Sample Program 5A

The WRITE #n statement in line 55 writes the record to the sequential file PART.DAT in a format that is consistent with the INPUT #n statement. Figure 5-11 shows the format of the data written to PART.DAT by Sample Program 5A.

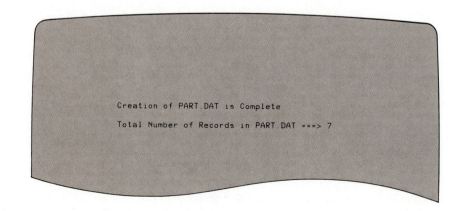

FIGURE 5-11
A listing of PART.DAT created by Sample Program 5A

In the Wrap-Up module, line 65 closes PART.DAT. This ensures that the last record entered by the operator is physically written to the data file on auxiliary storage. Figure 5-12 shows the display due to lines 66 through 69 of the Wrap-Up module.

FIGURE 5-12
The display due to the execution of the Wrap-Up module in Sample Program 5A

READING DATA FROM A SEQUENTIAL DATA FILE

he INPUT #n statement is used to read data from a data file that has been created by using the WRITE #n statement. The EOF function is used to determine when all the records have been processed. The following sections describe how the INPUT #n statement and EOF function work.

The INPUT #n Statement

The INPUT #n statement is similar to the READ statement except that it reads data from a data file instead of from DATA statements. In the following partial program,

```
OPEN "PART.DAT" FOR INPUT AS #1
        .
        .
        .
    INPUT #1, Part.No$, Description$, On.Hand, Wholesale
```

the PC reads four data items from the sequential file PART.DAT.

The general form of the INPUT #n statement is shown in Figure 5-13.

```
INPUT #filenumber, variable₁,, variable₂, ..., variableₙ
```

FIGURE 5-13   The general form of the INPUT #n statement

The EOF Function

When a sequential data file that was opened for output is closed, the PC automatically adds an end-of-file mark after the last record written to the file. Later, when the same sequential file is opened for input, you can use the EOF(n) function to test for the end-of-file mark. The n indicates the filenumber assigned to the file in the OPEN statement.

If the EOF function senses the end-of-file mark, it returns a value of –1 (true). Otherwise, it returns a value of 0 (false). Hence, the EOF function can be used in a DO WHILE statement to control the loop. For example, consider the partial program in Figure 5-14. In the DO WHILE statement, the EOF(1) function is used to control the Do loop. Each time the DO WHILE statement is executed, the PC checks to see whether the data pointer is pointing to the end-of-file mark in PART.DAT.

```
OPEN "PART.DAT" FOR INPUT AS #1
    .
    .
    .
DO WHILE NOT EOF(1)
    INPUT #1, Part.No$, Description$, On.Hand, Wholesale
    LET Record.Count = Record.Count + 1
    LET Total.On.Hand = Total.On.Hand + On.Hand
    LET Part.Cost = On.Hand * Wholesale
    LET Total.Part.Cost = Total.Part.Cost + Part.Cost
    LPRINT USING DL1$; Part.No$; Description$; On.Hand; Wholesale; Part.Cost
LOOP
```

FIGURE 5-14   Using the EOF function to test for end-of-file

When using the EOF function, it is important to organize your program so that the test for the end-of-file precedes the execution of the INPUT #n statement. In Figure 5-14, notice that only one INPUT #n statement is employed, and that this statement is placed inside at the top of the Do loop. This is different from our previous programs which employed two READ statements—one prior to the Do-While loop and one at the bottom of the Do-While loop.

The logic in Figure 5-14 also works when the file is empty (that is, when the file contains no records). If the PART.DAT file is empty, the OPEN statement in the partial program still opens the file for input. However, when the DO WHILE statement is executed, the EOF function immediately detects the end-of-file mark on the empty file, thereby causing control to pass to the statement following the corresponding LOOP statement.

SAMPLE PROGRAM 5B — PROCESSING A SEQUENTIAL DATA FILE

*I*n this sample program we will show how to read data and generate a report using the part file (PART.DAT) built by Sample Program 5A. The display shown in Figure 5-15A instructs the user to prepare the printer to receive the report. The report shown in Figure 5-15B contains a detail line for each part number. The total cost for each part is determined by multiplying the number of on hand by the wholesale price.

As part of the end-of-job routine, the sample program prints the number of part records processed, total number of parts in inventory, and the total cost of all the parts.

A. SCREEN DISPLAY

```
Set the paper in the printer to the top of page.

Press the Enter key when the printer is ready...

End of Job
```

B. PRINTED REPORT

```
                    Part Cost Report

       Part                                Wholesale      Part
       No.     Description     On Hand     Price          Cost
       ----    -----------     -------     ---------      ----
       323     Canon PC-25          12        799.92    9,599.04
       432     Timex Watch          53         27.95    1,481.35
       567     12 Inch Monitor      34         50.30    1,710.20
       578     Epson Printer        23        179.95    4,138.85
       745     6 Inch Frying P      17          9.71      165.07
       812     Mr. Coffee           39         21.90      854.10
       923     4-Piece Toaster       7         17.57      122.99
                                -------                ---------
                                    185                18,071.60

       Total Number of Parts =====>     7

       End of Job
```

FIGURE 5-15   **The screen display (A) and printed report (B) generated by Sample Program 5B**

A top-down chart, a program flowchart for each module, a program solution, and a discussion of the program solution follow.

Top-Down Chart and Program Flowcharts

Figure 5-16 illustrates the top-down chart and corresponding program flowcharts for each module in Sample Program 5B.

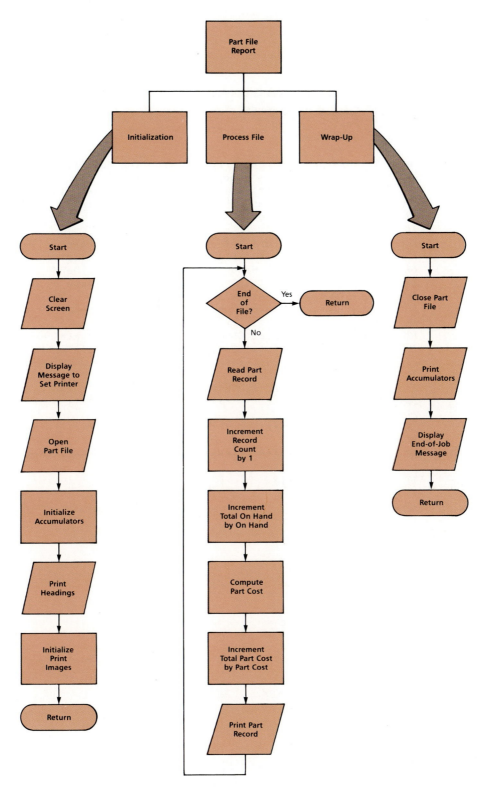

FIGURE 5-16 A top-down chart and corresponding program flowcharts
for Sample Program 5B

The QuickBASIC Program

The program in Figure 5-17 corresponds to the top-down chart and program flowcharts in Figure 5-16.

FIGURE 5-17
Sample Program 5B

```
 1   ' **************************************************************
 2   ' *   Sample Program 5B                    September 15, 1994  *
 3   ' *   Part File Report                                         *
 4   ' *   J. S. Quasney                                            *
 5   ' *                                                            *
 6   ' *   This program reads records from the data file PART.DAT   *
 7   ' *   and generates a report on the printer.                   *
 8   ' *       The number of part records processed, total pieces   *
 9   ' *   in inventory, and the total cost are printed as part of  *
10   ' *   the Wrap-Up module.                                      *
11   ' *                                                            *
12   ' *   Variables:  Part.No$        -- Part number               *
13   ' *               Description$     -- Part description          *
14   ' *               On.Hand          -- Number on hand            *
15   ' *               Total.On.Hand    -- Total pieces on hand      *
16   ' *               Wholesale        -- Wholesale price of part   *
17   ' *               Record.Count     -- Count of records added to *
18   ' *                                   PART.DAT                  *
19   ' *               Part.Cost        -- Cost of parts             *
20   ' *               Total.Cost.Part  -- Cost of all parts         *
21   ' *               Control$         -- Response when printer is  *
22   ' *                                   ready                     *
23   ' *               DL1$, TL1$, TL2$, TL3$, TL4$  -- Print Images *
24   ' **************************************************************
25
26   ' **************************************************************
27   ' *                        Main Module                         *
28   ' **************************************************************
29   GOSUB Initialization
30   GOSUB Process.File
31   GOSUB Wrap.Up
32   END
33
```

FIGURE 5-17
(continued)

```
34  ' ******************************************************************
35  ' *                        Initialization                        *
36  ' ******************************************************************
37  Initialization:
38      CLS   ' Clear Screen
39      LOCATE 10, 20
40      PRINT "Set the paper in the printer to the top of page."
41      LOCATE 12, 20
42      INPUT "Press the Enter key when the printer is ready...", Control$
43      OPEN "B:PART.DAT" FOR INPUT AS #1
44      Record.Count = 0
45      Total.On.Hand = 0
46      Total.Part.Cost = 0
47      LPRINT "            Part Cost Report"
48      LPRINT
49      LPRINT "Part                              Wholesale      Part"
50      LPRINT "No.      Description      On Hand  Price          Cost"
51      LPRINT "----     -----------      -------  ---------      ----"
52      DL1$ = "\ \         \          \  #,###    #,###.## ##,###.##"
53      TL1$ = "                        -------            ---------"
54      TL2$ = "                        ##,###            ###,###.##"
55      TL3$ = "Total Number of Parts ====>#,###"
56      TL4$ = "End of Job"
57  RETURN
58
59  ' ******************************************************************
60  ' *                        Process File                          *
61  ' ******************************************************************
62  Process.File:
63      DO WHILE NOT EOF(1)
64          INPUT #1, Part.No$, Description$, On.Hand, Wholesale
65          LET Record.Count = Record.Count + 1
66          LET Total.On.Hand = Total.On.Hand + On.Hand
67          LET Part.Cost = On.Hand * Wholesale
68          LET Total.Part.Cost = Total.Part.Cost + Part.Cost
69          LPRINT USING DL1$; Part.No$; Description$; On.Hand; Wholesale; Part.Cost
70      LOOP
71  RETURN
72
73  ' ******************************************************************
74  ' *                          Wrap-Up                             *
75  ' ******************************************************************
76  Wrap.Up:
77      CLOSE #1
78      LPRINT TL1$
79      LPRINT USING TL2$; Total.On.Hand; Total.Part.Cost
80      LPRINT
81      LPRINT USING TL3$; Record.Count
82      LPRINT
83      LPRINT TL4$
84      LOCATE 14, 20
85      PRINT "End of Job"
86  RETURN
87
88  ' ******************** End of Program ********************
```

Discussion of the Program Solution

When Sample Program 5B is executed, the screen display and printed report shown earlier in Figure 5-15 on page QB 92 are generated. The following points should be considered in the program solution represented by Sample Program 5B in Figure 5-17.

- Lines 39 through 42 in the Initialization module display on the screen instructions to the user to set the paper in the printer and press the Enter key when ready. Notice how the INPUT statement in line 42 temporarily halts the program until the user has prepared the printer to receive the report.
- Line 43 opens the data file PART.DAT on the B drive for input as filenumber 1. Hence, the program can read records from B:PART.DAT.
- The DO WHILE statement in line 63 controls the Do-While loop using a condition made up of the EOF function. The loop continues to execute while it is not end-of-file.
- Within the Do-While loop, the INPUT #n statement in line 64 reads a PART.DAT record by referencing filenumber 1 which was specified in the OPEN statement (line 43). After lines 65 through 68 manipulate the data and accumulate totals, line 69 prints the detail line. Line 70 returns control to the DO WHILE statement in line 63 which tests for the end-of-file mark.
- When the end-of-file mark is sensed in line 63, control passes to the RETURN statement in line 71. Line 71 returns control to line 31 in the Main module. Line 31 calls the Wrap-Up module, which prints the accumulators and displays an end-of-job message on the screen. Finally, control returns to the END statement in line 32 and the program terminates execution.

TRY IT YOURSELF EXERCISES

1. Fill in the blanks in the following sentences:
   a. The _____ statement with a mode of _____ must be executed before an INPUT #n statement is executed.
   b. The _____ statement must be executed before a WRITE #n statement is executed.
   c. The _____ function is used to test for the end-of-file mark with a sequential data file.
   d. When records are to be added to the end of a sequential data file, the _____ mode is used in the OPEN statement.

2. Assume Cost = 15, Desc$ = Keyboard, and Code = 4. Using commas, quotation marks, and ↵ for end of record, indicate the makeup of the record written to auxiliary storage by the following WRITE #n statement:

   ```
   WRITE #1, Cost, Desc$, Code
   ```

3. Explain why the EOF function should be used in a condition controlling the loop before the INPUT #n statement is executed.

4. A program is to read records from one of three sequential data files: PART1.DAT, PART2.DAT, and PART3.DAT. The three files are stored on the diskette in the A drive. Write three OPEN statements that would allow the program to read records from any of the three sequential files.

5. Which of the following are invalid file-handling statements? Why?
   a. OPEN Seq$ FOR OUTPUT AS #1
   b. INPUT #1, Cost,
   c. DO WHILE NOT EOF(#2)
   d. CLOSE #1
   e. WRITE #2, A,
   f. OPEN FOR INPUT "INV.DAT" AS #2
   g. WRITE #1, USING "####.##"; Cost

STUDENT ASSIGNMENTS

STUDENT ASSIGNMENT 1: Payroll File Build

Instructions: Design and code a top-down QuickBASIC program to build the payroll file PAYROLL.DAT. Use the sample data shown under INPUT. Generate a screen to receive the data similar to the one under OUTPUT. At the end-of-job, display the number of records written to the data file.

INPUT: Use the following sample data:

EMPLOYEE NUMBER	EMPLOYEE NAME	DEPENDENTS	PAY RATE	HOURS WORKED
23A5	Linda Frat	3	6.75	40
45K8	Joe Smit	1	12.50	38.5
56T1	Lisa Ann	1	16.25	48
65R4	Jeff Max	5	17.75	42
73E6	Susan Dex	2	13.50	40
87Q2	Jeff Web	0	22.45	50
91W2	Marci Jean	3	13.45	40
92R4	Jodi Lin	9	11.50	56
94Y2	Amanda Jo	12	12.75	20
96Y7	Niki Rai	3	16.00	42.5

OUTPUT: The sequential data file PAYROLL.DAT is created in auxiliary storage. The results for the first payroll record are shown below on the left. The results below on the right are displayed prior to termination of the program.

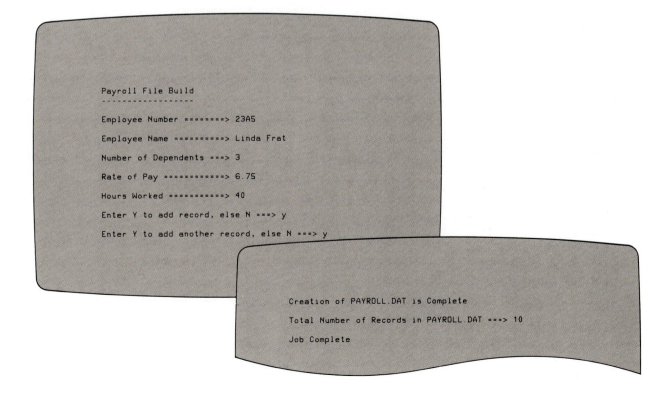

```
Payroll File Build
------------------

Employee Number ========> 23A5

Employee Name ==========> Linda Frat

Number of Dependents ===> 3

Rate of Pay ============> 6.75

Hours Worked ===========> 40

Enter Y to add record, else N ===> y

Enter Y to add another record, else N ===> y
```

```
Creation of PAYROLL.DAT is Complete

Total Number of Records in PAYROLL.DAT ===> 10

Job Complete
```

STUDENT ASSIGNMENT 2: Processing a Payroll File

Instructions: Design and code a top-down QuickBASIC program that generates the messages shown on the screen display under OUTPUT and prints the payroll report under OUTPUT. Apply the following conditions:

1. Gross pay = hours worked × hourly rate.
   Overtime (hours worked > 40) are paid at 1.5 times the hourly rate.
2. Federal withholding tax = 0.2 × (gross pay – dependents × 38.46). Assign federal withholding tax a value of zero if the gross pay less the product of the number of dependents and $38.46 is negative.
3. Net pay = gross pay – federal withholding tax.
4. At the end-of-job, print the number of employees processed, total gross pay, total federal withholding tax, and total net pay.
5. Print the report on the printer.

INPUT: Use the sequential data file PAYROLL.DAT created in Student Assignment 1. If you did not do Student Assignment 1, ask your instructor for a copy of PAYROLL.DAT.

OUTPUT: The following screen with messages and prompts is displayed:

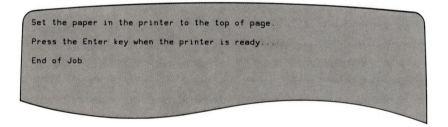

```
Set the paper in the printer to the top of page.

Press the Enter key when the printer is ready...

End of Job
```

The following report prints on the printer:

```
                         Payroll File List

        Emp.                        Pay
        No.    Name     Dep.  Hours  Rate  Gross Pay  With. Tax  Net Pay
        ----   ----     ----  -----  ----  ---------  ---------  -------
        23A5   Linda Frat  3   40.0   6.75    270.00      30.92   239.08
        45K8   Joe Smit    1   38.5  12.50    481.25      88.56   392.69
        56T1   Lisa Ann    1   48.0  16.25    845.00     161.31   683.69
        6SR4   Jeff Max    5   42.0  17.75    763.25     114.19   649.06
        73E6   Susan Dex   2   40.0  13.50    540.00      92.62   447.38
        87Q2   Jeff Web    0   50.0  22.45  1,234.75     246.95   987.80
        91W2   Marci Jean  3   40.0  13.45    538.00      84.52   453.48
        92R4   Jodi Lin    9   56.0  11.50    736.00      77.97   658.03
        94Y2   Amanda Jo  12   20.0  12.75    255.00       0.00   255.00
        96Y7   Niki Rai    3   42.5  16.00    700.00     116.92   583.08

        Total Employees =======>       10
        Total Gross Pay =======>  6,363.25
        Total Tax =============>  1,013.97
        Total Net Pay =========>  5,349.28

        End of Payroll Report
```

PROJECT 6

Arrays and Functions

*I*n the previous projects we used simple variables such as Count, Emp.Name$, and Balance to store and access data in a program. In this project we discuss variables that can store more than one value under the same name. Variables that can hold more than one value at a time are called **arrays**.

An array is often used to store a **table** of organized data. Income tax tables, insurance tables, or sales tax tables are examples of tables that can be stored in an array for processing purposes. Once the table elements are assigned to an array, the array can be searched to extract the proper values.

Functions are used to handle common mathematical and string operations. For example, it is often necessary in programming to obtain the square root of a number or extract a substring from a string of characters. Without functions, these types of operations would require that you write sophisticated routines in your program. Functions clearly simplify the programming task.

Although we discuss only the most frequently used functions, you should be aware that QuickBASIC has over 70 built-in functions to aid you in your programming. For a summary of all the functions available in QuickBASIC, refer to pages R.4 and R.5 of the reference card in the back of this book.

ARRAYS

*T*he banking application in Figure 6-1 illustrates an example of table processing. The account number, name of the account holder, and account balance of individuals who have savings are stored in arrays. When the teller enters account number 20013, the program searches the account number array to find an equal account number.

When the equal account number is found, the corresponding name (Darla Simmons) and the corresponding balance (932.49) are *pulled* from the table and displayed on the screen.

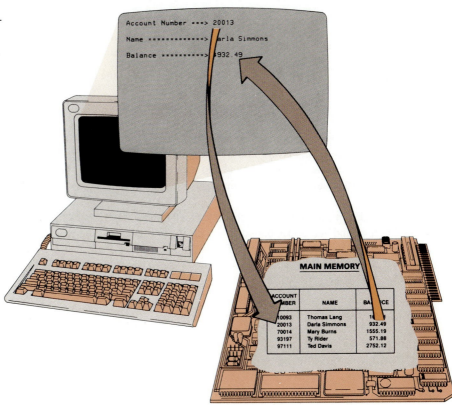

FIGURE 6-1
An example of table processing

THE DIM STATEMENT

efore arrays can be used, they must be declared in a program. This is the purpose of the DIM statement, also called the dimension statement. The general form of the DIM statement is shown in Figure 6-2.

DIM array-name(lb$_1$ TO ub$_1$), ..., array-name(lb$_1$ TO ub$_n$)

where **array-name** is a variable name, **lb$_1$** is a positive or negative integer or numeric variable that serves as the lower-bound value of the array, and **ub$_n$** is a positive or negative integer or numeric variable that serves as the upper-bound value of the array.

FIGURE 6-2 **The general form of the DIM statement**

Figure 6-3 illustrates several examples of declaring arrays. Example 1 reserves storage for a one-dimensional numeric array Tax, which consists of 5 elements, or storage locations. These elements—Tax(1), Tax(2), Tax(3), Tax(4), and Tax(5)—can be used in a program the same way in which a simple variable can be used. Notice that the elements of an array are distinguished from one another by **subscripts** that follow the array name within parentheses.

EXAMPLE	DIM STATEMENT
1	DIM Tax(1 TO 5)
2	DIM Job.Code$(1 TO 15), Bonus(1 TO 15)
3	DIM Part.No$(Begin TO Fin), Des(Begin TO Fin)
4	DIM Function.Tax(1 TO 50, 1 TO 25)
5	DIM Inventory.No$(15 TO 35)
6	DIM X(-5 TO 10)

FIGURE 6-3 **Examples of the DIM statement**

Example 2 in Figure 6-3 declares two arrays—Job.Code$ and Bonus. Both arrays are declared to have 15 elements. Thus, Job.Code$(1) through Job.Code$(15) and Bonus(1) through Bonus(15) can be referenced in the program containing the DIM statement. Job.Code$(0) and Job.Code$(16) do not exist according to the DIM statement, and therefore, should not be referenced. You may declare as many arrays in a DIM statement as required by the program.

Example 3 illustrates that the lower-bound and upper-bound values can be variables that are assigned a value prior to the execution of the DIM statement. Example 4 illustrates a two-dimensional array. QuickBASIC allows an array to have up to 60 dimensions.

Examples 5 and 6 in Figure 6-3 show that the lower-bound of an array can be a value different from 1. It is important to note that the lower-bound and upper-bound values define the range of the array. Any subscript reference that is outside the range will cause a diagnostic message to display.

SAMPLE PROGRAM 6 — CUSTOMER ACCOUNT TABLE LOOKUP

*I*n this sample program we implement the banking application shown on page QB 99 in Figure 6-1. The account number, name of the account holder, and account balance of customers who have savings accounts are shown in Figure 6-4. The table data is stored in the sequential data file ACCOUNTS.DAT. ACCOUNTS.DAT includes a data item (5) prior to the first account record that is equal to the number of records in the data file.

ACCOUNT NUMBER	CUSTOMER NAME	BALANCE
10093	Thomas Lang	$ 100.51
20013	Darla Simmons	932.49
70014	Mary Burns	1,555.19
93197	Ty Rider	571.88
97111	Ted Davis	2,752.12

FIGURE 6-4   The table data stored in ACCOUNTS.DAT

The screen display in Figure 6-5 illustrates the output results when the user enters account number 70014. When the user enters the account number, the program should direct the PC to *look up* and display the corresponding customer name and balance. The message at the bottom of the screen in Figure 6-5 asks the user to enter the letter Y to look up another account or the letter N to terminate the program.

If the account number is not found in the table, a diagnostic error displays.

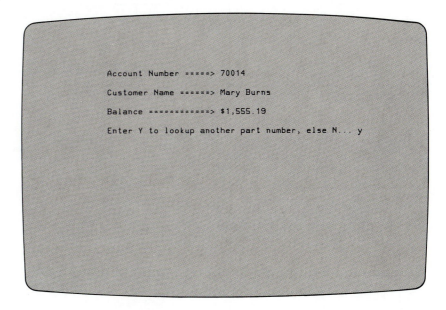

FIGURE 6-5
The display due to the execution of Sample Program 6 and the entering of account number 70014

```
Account Number ======> 70014

Customer Name ======> Mary Burns

Balance ============> $1,555.19

Enter Y to lookup another part number, else N... y
```

A top-down chart, a program flowchart for each module, a program solution, and a discussion of the program solution follow.

Top-Down Chart and Program Flowcharts

The top-down chart and corresponding program flowcharts that illustrate the logic for the Sample Program 6 are shown in Figure 6-6.

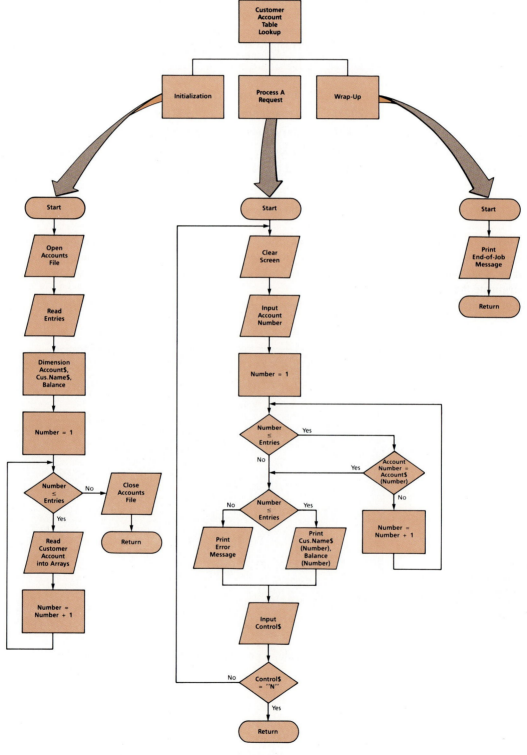

FIGURE 6-6 A top-down chart and corresponding program flowcharts for Sample Program 6

In the Initialization module in Figure 6-6, ACCOUNTS.DAT is opened and the number of records in the account file is read. This value is used to dimension the three arrays that will hold the account information. Next, the same value is used to control a Do-While loop that assigns the account information to the three arrays. After the Do-While loop is finished, ACCOUNTS.DAT is closed.

In the Process A Request module, the program accepts the account number from the user. A Do-While loop is then used to search the array that contains the account numbers. If the search is successful, the customer name and balance display. If the search is unsuccessful, a diagnostic message displays. Finally, the user is asked if he or she wants to enter another account number.

When the user enters the letter N (or n), control returns to the Main module and the Wrap-Up module displays an end-of-job message.

The QuickBASIC Program

The QuickBASIC code in Figure 6-7 corresponds to the top box in the top-down chart in Figure 6-6. The GOSUB statements call the subordinate modules. Following the return of control from the Wrap-Up module, the END statement terminates execution of the program.

```
23  ' ***************************************************************
24  ' *                        Main Module                         *
25  ' ***************************************************************
26  GOSUB Initialization
27  GOSUB Process.Request
28  GOSUB Wrap.Up
29  END
```

FIGURE 6-7   **The Main module for Sample Program 6**

Initialization Module   The Initialization module for Sample Program 6 is shown in Figure 6-8. The primary objective of this module is to load the data in ACCOUNTS.DAT into the arrays. Line 35 opens ACCOUNTS.DAT on the B drive. Line 36 assigns the first data item in ACCOUNTS.DAT to the variable Entries. Entries is then assigned the value 5. Line 37 dimensions the three arrays with an upper-bound value equal to Entries. The For loop in lines 38 through 40 reads the data in ACCOUNTS.DAT into the three arrays. Arrays Account$, Cus.Name$, and Balance, therefore contain the data in ACCOUNTS.DAT. Since each array contains data that corresponds to the other arrays, we call them **parallel arrays**. Line 41 closes ACCOUNTS.DAT before control is returned to the Main module.

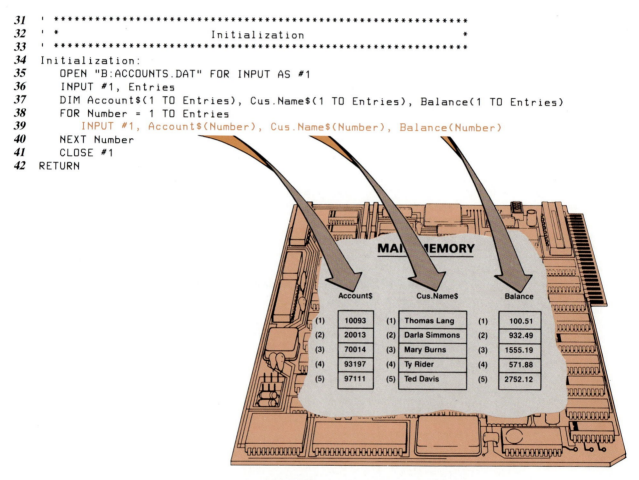

```
31  ' ****************************************************************
32  ' *                        Initialization                       *
33  ' ****************************************************************
34  Initialization:
35      OPEN "B:ACCOUNTS.DAT" FOR INPUT AS #1
36      INPUT #1, Entries
37      DIM Account$(1 TO Entries), Cus.Name$(1 TO Entries), Balance(1 TO Entries)
38      FOR Number = 1 TO Entries
39          INPUT #1, Account$(Number), Cus.Name$(Number), Balance(Number)
40      NEXT Number
41      CLOSE #1
42  RETURN
```

FIGURE 6-8   The Initialization module for Sample Program 6

Process A Request Module   After the data in ACCOUNTS.DAT is loaded into the arrays and control passes back to the Main module, line 27 transfers control to the Process A Request module (Figure 6-9). This module begins by clearing the screen and accepting the account number from the user. The account number is assigned to the variable Search.Argument$ (line 51).

```
44  ' **********************************************************
45  ' *                    Process A Request                   *
46  ' **********************************************************
47  Process.Request:
48      DO
49          CLS   ' Clear Screen
50          LOCATE 5, 15
51          INPUT "Account Number =====> ", Search.Argument$
52          FOR Number = 1 TO Entries
53              IF Search.Argument$ = Account$(Number) THEN
54                  EXIT FOR    ' Process a Table Hit
55              END IF
56          NEXT Number
57          IF Number <= Entries THEN
58              LOCATE 7, 15
59              PRINT "Customer Name ======> "; Cus.Name$(Number)
60              LOCATE 9, 15
61              PRINT USING "Balance =============> $$,###.##"; Balance(Number)
62          ELSE
63              LOCATE 7, 15
64              PRINT "Account Number "; Search.Argument$; " NOT FOUND"
65          END IF
66          LOCATE 11, 15
67          INPUT "Enter Y to lookup another part number, else N... ", Control$
68      LOOP UNTIL Control$ = "N" OR Control$ = "n"
69  RETURN
```

FIGURE 6-9   The Process A Request module for Sample Program 6

The For loop in lines 52 through 56 of Figure 6-9 searches the Account$ array for a match with Search.Argument$. Each time through the loop, the IF statement (line 53) compares Search.Argument$ to the next element in Account$ until a *hit* is made. When a *hit* occurs, the EXIT FOR statement in line 54 causes a premature exit from the For loop and control passes to line 57. If no *hit* occurs, a normal exit from the For loop also passes control to line 57.

Line 57 determines if the search for the account number in Account$ was successful. If the search was successful, then Number is less than or equal to Entries. In this case, the customer number and balance from the two corresponding arrays are displayed using the value of Number for the subscript. Figure 6-10 shows the display due to a successful search.

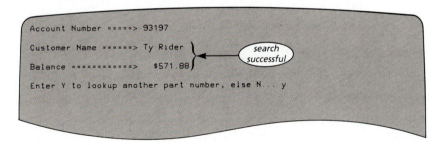

FIGURE 6-10   The display from Sample Program 6 due to entering the account number 93197

If the search is unsuccessful, then Number is greater than Entries and the diagnostic message in line 64 displays as shown in Figure 6-11. Note that if there is a premature exit from the For loop, the search is successful. If the For loop ends normally, the search is unsuccessful.

FIGURE 6-11

The display from Sample Program 6 due to entering the invalid account number 12123

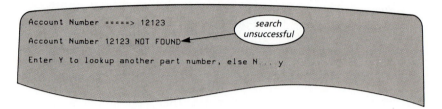

```
Account Number =====> 12123

Account Number 12123 NOT FOUND          search
                                        unsuccessful

Enter Y to lookup another part number, else N... y
```

After the true or false task in the IF statement (lines 57 through 65) is executed, line 67 requests that the user enter the letter Y to process another account number or the letter N to terminate execution of the program.

The complete QuickBASIC program is shown in Figure 6-12.

FIGURE 6-12

Sample Program 6

```
 1  ' **********************************************************************
 2  ' *  Sample Program 6                        September 15, 1994   *
 3  ' *  Customer Account Table Lookup                                *
 4  ' *  J. S. Quasney                                                *
 5  ' *                                                               *
 6  ' *  This program loads the data in ACCOUNTS.DAT into arrays.     *
 7  ' *  The user enters the account number and the program looks     *
 8  ' *  up and displays the customer number and account balance.     *
 9  ' *          If the account number is not found, then a           *
10  ' *  diagnostic message is displayed.  After processing a         *
11  ' *  request, the user is asked if he or she wishes to            *
12  ' *  display information of another account or terminate the      *
13  ' *  program.                                                     *
14  ' *                                                               *
15  ' *  Variables: Account$        -- Account number array           *
16  ' *             Cus.Name$       -- Customer name array            *
17  ' *             Balance         -- Customer balance array         *
18  ' *             Search.Argument$ -- Account number requested      *
19  ' *             Control$        -- Response to continue           *
20  ' *             Entries         -- Number of customers            *
21  ' **********************************************************************
22
23  ' **********************************************************************
24  ' *                        Main Module                            *
25  ' **********************************************************************
26  GOSUB Initialization
27  GOSUB Process.Request
28  GOSUB Wrap.Up
29  END
30
```

FIGURE 6-12
(continued)

```
31  ' ***************************************************************
32  ' *                      Initialization                       *
33  ' ***************************************************************
34  Initialization:
35      OPEN "B:ACCOUNTS.DAT" FOR INPUT AS #1
36      INPUT #1, Entries
37      DIM Account$(1 TO Entries), Cus.Name$(1 TO Entries), Balance(1 TO Entries)
38      FOR Number = 1 TO Entries
39          INPUT #1, Account$(Number), Cus.Name$(Number), Balance(Number)
40      NEXT Number
41      CLOSE #1
42  RETURN
43
44  ' ***************************************************************
45  ' *                     Process A Request                     *
46  ' ***************************************************************
47  Process.Request:
48      DO
49          CLS  ' Clear Screen
50          LOCATE 5, 15
51          INPUT "Account Number =====> ", Search.Argument$
52          FOR Number = 1 TO Entries
53              IF Search.Argument$ = Account$(Number) THEN
54                  EXIT FOR   ' Process a Table Hit
55              END IF
56          NEXT Number
57          IF Number <= Entries THEN
58              LOCATE 7, 15
59              PRINT "Customer Name ======> "; Cus.Name$(Number)
60              LOCATE 9, 15
61              PRINT USING "Balance ============> $$,###.##"; Balance(Number)
62          ELSE
63              LOCATE 7, 15
64              PRINT "Account Number "; Search.Argument$; " NOT FOUND"
65          END IF
66          LOCATE 11, 15
67          INPUT "Enter Y to lookup another part number, else N... ", Control$
68      LOOP UNTIL Control$ = "N" OR Control$ = "n"
69  RETURN
70
71  ' ***************************************************************
72  ' *                        Wrap-Up                            *
73  ' ***************************************************************
74  Wrap.Up:
75      LOCATE 13, 15
76      PRINT "Job Complete"
77  RETURN
78  ' ******************** End of Program ********************
```

FUNCTIONS

uickBASIC includes over 70 numeric and string functions. Numeric functions are used to handle common mathematical calculations. String functions are used to manipulate strings of characters.

Numeric Functions

Three of the most frequently used numeric functions are the INT, SQR, and RND functions. The purpose of these functions is summarized in Figure 6-13.

FUNCTION	FUNCTION VALUE
INT(X)	Returns the largest integer that is less than or equal to the argument X.
SQR(X)	Returns the square root of the argument X.
RND	Returns a random number greater than or equal to zero and less than 1.

FIGURE 6-13   Frequently used numeric functions

INT Function   The INT function returns a whole number that is less than or equal to the argument. Figure 6-14 shows several examples of the INT function.

VALUE OF VARIABLE	QuickBASIC STATEMENT	RESULT
X = 12.45	LET Y = INT(X)	Y = 12
H = 27.89	LET G = INT(H + 10)	G = 37
J = -15.67	LET K = INT(J)	K = -16

FIGURE 6-14   Examples of the INT function

SQR Function   The SQR function computes the square root of the argument. Figure 6-15 illustrates several examples of the SQR function. Note that the argument for the SQR function must be a non-negative value.

VALUE OF VARIABLE	QuickBASIC STATEMENT	RESULT
Y = 4	LET X = SQR(Y)	X = 2
D = 27	LET P = SQR(D * 3)	P = 9
E = -16	LET U = SQR(E)	Illegal Function Call

FIGURE 6-15   Examples of the SQR function

RND Function The RND function returns an unpredictable number that is greater than or equal to zero and less than 1. The partial program in Figure 6-16 uses a For loop and the RND function to generate three random numbers — .7132002, .6291881, and .3409873.

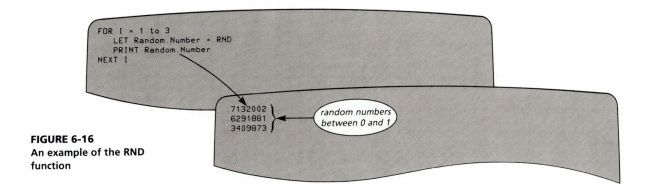

FIGURE 6-16
An example of the RND function

The INT and RND functions can be used to generate random digits over any range. The following expression generates random numbers between L and U:

```
INT((U - L + 1) * RND + L)
```

For example, to simulate the roll of a six-sided die, we can write the following:

```
LET Die = INT((6 - 1 + 1) * RND + 1)
```

   or

```
LET Die = INT(6 * RND + 1)
```

In Figure 6-17, the For loop generates five rolls of two dice. The first LET statement represents the roll of one die and the second LET statement represents the roll of the second die.

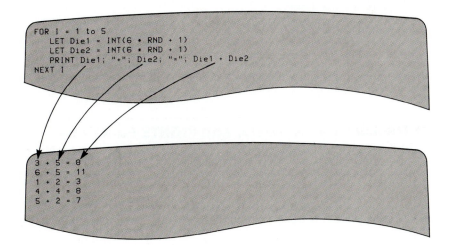

FIGURE 6-17
An example of a partial program that simulates five rolls of two dice

Each time you run the program in Figure 6-17, it generates the same sequence of random numbers. To generate a new sequence of random numbers each time you execute the program, insert the RANDOMIZE statement at the top of the program. When executed, the RANDOMIZE statement requests that you enter a number between –32768 and 32767. The value you enter is used by the PC to develop a new set of random numbers.

String Functions

The capability to process strings is important in business applications. In QuickBASIC, you can join two strings together through the use of the concatenation operator (+). For example, the following LET statement:

```
LET Join$ = "ABC" + "DEF"
```

assigns the variable Join$ the value ABCDEF. Besides the concatenation operator, QuickBASIC includes over 25 functions that allow you to manipulate string values.

The most frequently used string functions are shown in Figure 6-18.

FUNCTION	FUNCTION VALUE
DATE$	Returns the system date as a string in the form mm-dd-yyyy.
LEFT$(S$, X)	Returns the leftmost X characters of the string argument S$.
LEN(S$)	Returns the number of characters in the string argument S$.
MID$(S$, P, X)	Returns X characters from the string argument S$ beginning at position P.
RIGHT$(S$, X)	Returns the rightmost X characters of the string argument S$.
TIME$	Returns the system time of day as a string in the form HH:MM:SS.

FIGURE 6-18   Frequently used string functions

The DATE$ and TIME$ Functions   The DATE$ and TIME$ functions return the DOS system date and time. For example, if the system date is initialized to September 15, 1994, then the statement PRINT "The date is "; DATE$ displays the following result:

```
The date is 09-15-1994
```

If the system time is equal to 11:44:42, then the statement PRINT "The time is "; TIME$ displays the following result:

```
The time is 11:44:42
```

The system time is maintained in 24-hour notation. That is, 1:30 P.M. displays as 13:30:00.

Use of the LEFT$, LEN, MID$, and RIGHT$ Functions

The LEN(S$) function returns the number of characters in S$. For example, the following LET statement assigns Length the value 5 because there are 5 characters in the string BASIC:

```
LET Length = LEN("BASIC")
```

The LET statement LET Number = LEN(DATE$) assigns Number the value 10 because there are 10 characters in the system date (mm/dd/yyyy).

The LEFT$, MID$, and RIGHT$ functions are used to extract substrings from a string. Figure 6-19 illustrates several examples of these functions.

VALUE OF VARIABLE	QuickBASIC STATEMENT	RESULT
Assume S$ is equal to GOTO is a four-letter word		
1	LET Q$ = LEFT$(S$, 7)	Q$ = GOTO is
2	LET W$ = LEFT$(S$, 4)	W$ = GOTO
3	LET D$ = RIGHT$(S$, 11)	D$ = letter word
4	LET K$ = RIGHT$(S$, 1)	K$ = d
5	LET M$ = MID$(S$, 6, 2)	M$ = is
6	LET T$ = MID$(S$, 16, 6)	T$ = letter

FIGURE 6-19   Examples of the LEFT$, RIGHT$, and MID$ functions

QuickBASIC also allows the argument to include a function. For example, if the system date is 9/15/94, then the LET statement LET Day$ = MID$(DATE$, 4, 2) assigns Day$ the string value 15. If the system time is equal to 10:32:52, then the LET statement LET Second$ = MID$(Time$, 7, 2) assigns Second$ the string value 52.

Consider the partial program in Figure 6-20 and the corresponding output results. Lines 1 and 2 display the system date and time. Lines 4 through 6 display on separate lines the substrings month, day, and year. Lines 8 through 10 display on separate lines the substrings hour, minute, and second.

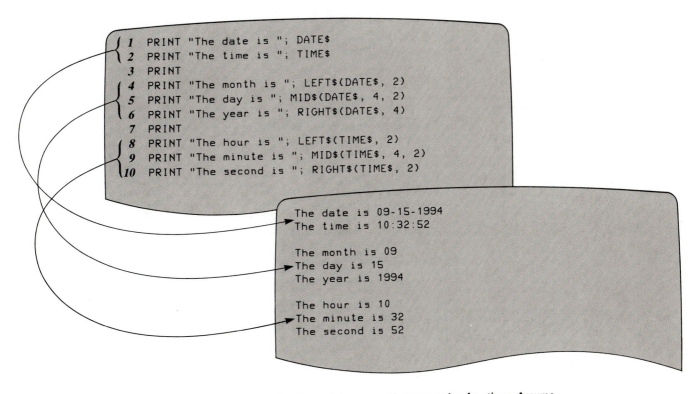

```
 1   PRINT "The date is "; DATE$
 2   PRINT "The time is "; TIME$
 3   PRINT
 4   PRINT "The month is "; LEFT$(DATE$, 2)
 5   PRINT "The day is "; MID$(DATE$, 4, 2)
 6   PRINT "The year is "; RIGHT$(DATE$, 4)
 7   PRINT
 8   PRINT "The hour is "; LEFT$(TIME$, 2)
 9   PRINT "The minute is "; MID$(TIME$, 4, 2)
10   PRINT "The second is "; RIGHT$(TIME$, 2)
```

```
The date is 09-15-1994
The time is 10:32:52

The month is 09
The day is 15
The year is 1994

The hour is 10
The minute is 32
The second is 52
```

FIGURE 6-20   An example of a partial program that uses string functions. Assume system date is 9/15/94 and system time is 10:32:52

TRY IT YOURSELF EXERCISES

1. What is displayed when the following programs are executed?

   a.
   ```
   ' Exercise 1.a
   City$ = "Los Angeles"
   PRINT LEFT$(City$, 1) + MID$(City$, 5, 1) + " LAW"
   END
   ```

   b.
   ```
   ' Exercise 1.b
   PRINT "Number", "Square", "Square Root"
   FOR I = 1 TO 10
       PRINT I, I ^ 2, SQR(I)
   NEXT I
   END
   ```

2. Assume arrays Part and Cost are dimensioned by the statement `DIM Part(1 TO 5), Cost(1 TO 5)`. Assume that the two arrays were loaded with the following values:

ARRAY PART	ARRAY COST
15	1.23
71	2.34
92	.25
94	1.37
99	5.25

   Indicate how you would reference the following values using subscripts. For example, .25 can be referenced by Cost(3).
   a. 71   b. 5.25   c. 2.34   d. 15   e. 1.37   f. 1.23   g. 99

3. Write a `DIM` statement to minimally dimension array X so that subscripts in the range 1 to 900 are valid and array Y so that subscripts in the range –5 to 22 are valid.

4. Given that array G has been declared to have 10 elements (1 to 10), assume that each element of G has a value. Write a partial program that includes a `DIM` statement to shift all the values up one location. That is, assign G(1) to G(2), G(2) to G(3), and G(10) to G(1).

5. Identify the errors, if any, in each of the following:
   a. `DIM Amt(1 TO -1)`
   b. `DIM Bal (1 TOO 10)`
   c. `DIM Sales`
   d. `DIM (1 TO 35)X`

6. Indicate what each of the following are equal to. Assume Phrase$ is equal to `Aim the arrow carefully`.
   a. `LEN(Phrase$)`
   b. `MID$(Phrase$, 4, 3)`
   c. `LEFT$(Phrase$, 13)`
   d. `RIGHT$(Phrase$, 5)`

7. Assume that the system date is equal to December 25, 1994 and the system time is equal to 11:12:15. Evaluate the following:
   a. `X$ = TIME$`
   b. `X$ = MID$(TIME$, 4, 1)`
   c. `X$ = RIGHT$(DATE$, 2)`
   d. `X$ = LEFT$(DATE$, 2)`

8. Write a LET statement that assigns Number a random value between 1 and 52.
9. Explain the purpose of the RANDOMIZE statement.
10. What does each of the following equal?
    a. INT(23.46)
    b. SQR(121)
    c. LEN("ABC")
    d. INT(-12.43)
    e. SQR(SQR(81))
    f. SQR(INT(36.57))

STUDENT ASSIGNMENTS

STUDENT ASSIGNMENT 1: Phone Number Lookup

Instructions: Design and code a top-down QuickBASIC program that requests a person's last name and displays the person's telephone number.

Read the data shown in the phone number table under INPUT into parallel arrays from a sequential data file or DATA statements. If you plan to use a sequential data file, ask your instructor for a copy of PHONE.DAT.

Accept a person's last name in lowercase from the user. Search the last name array. If the search is successful, display the corresponding telephone number. If the search is unsuccessful, display a diagnostic message. After the search, ask the user if he or she wants to look up another telephone number. The output results should be similar to the displayed results shown under OUTPUT.

INPUT: Use the following phone number table data. Include a value at the beginning of the file which indicates the number of elements required in the parallel arrays that will hold the names and phone numbers.

Look up the phone numbers of the following individuals: fuqua, bingle, smith, and course.

NAME	PHONE NUMBER
miller	(213) 430-2865
flaming	(213) 866-9082
fuqua	(714) 925-3391
bingle	(805) 402-3376
course	(213) 423-7765

OUTPUT: The following results are displayed for bingle and smith:

```
Person's Name =====> bingle
Phone Number =====> (805) 402-3376
Enter Y to lookup another phone number, Else N... y
```

```
Person's Name =====> smith
The Name smith NOT FOUND
Enter Y to lookup another phone number, Else N... y
```

STUDENT ASSIGNMENT 2: Weight Table Lookup

Instructions: Design and code a top-down QuickBASIC program that accepts a male or female height and displays the average weight ranges for a small-framed, medium-framed, and large-framed person. If the search is unsuccessful, display an error message. The table entries are shown in the height and weight table data under INPUT. The output results are shown under OUTPUT.

INPUT: Use the following height and weight table data. Read the table data into two separate sets of parallel arrays, one for the male weights and one for the female weights, by means of a data file or DATA statements. If you plan to use a sequential data file, ask your instructor for a copy of WEIGHT.DAT. Initialize a variable to nine (the number of different heights for males and for females prior to the DIM statement). Use this variable to dimension the arrays and control any loops that search for heights. Look up the following:

Sex – Male, Height – 72
Sex – Female, Height – 64
Sex – Male, Height – 76
Sex – Female, Height – 72
Sex – Male, Height – 70

	HEIGHT	SMALL FRAME	MEDIUM FRAME	LARGE FRAME
M E N	66	124–133	130–143	138–156
	67	128–136	134–147	142–161
	68	132–141	138–152	147–168
	69	136–145	142–156	151–170
	70	140–150	146–160	155–174
	71	144–154	150–165	159–179
	72	148–158	154–170	164–184
	73	152–162	158–175	168–189
	74	156–167	162–180	173–194

	HEIGHT	SMALL FRAME	MEDIUM FRAME	LARGE FRAME
W O M E N	62	102–110	107–119	115–131
	63	105–113	110–122	118–134
	64	108–116	113–126	121–138
	65	111–119	116–130	125–142
	66	114–123	120–135	129–148
	67	118–127	124–139	133–150
	68	122–131	128–43	137–154
	69	126–135	132–147	141–158
	70	130–140	136–151	145–163

OUTPUT: The following screen displays for the first set of data under INPUT:

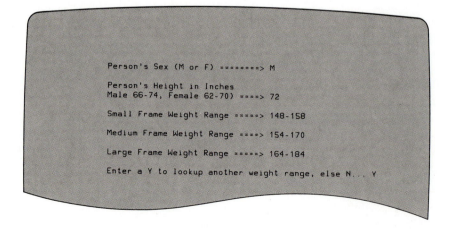

```
Person's Sex (M or F) ========> M

Person's Height in Inches
Male 66-74, Female 62-70) ====> 72

Small Frame Weight Range =====> 148-158

Medium Frame Weight Range ====> 154-170

Large Frame Weight Range =====> 164-184

Enter a Y to lookup another weight range, else N... Y
```

APPENDIX

QuickBASIC Debugging Techniques

Although the top-down approach and structured programming techniques help minimize errors, they by no means guarantee error-free programs. Owing to carelessness or insufficient thought, program portions can be constructed which do not work as anticipated and give erroneous results. When such problems occur, you need techniques to isolate the errors and correct the erroneous program statements.

QuickBASIC can detect many different **grammatical errors** and display appropriate diagnostic messages. However, there is no BASIC system that can detect all errors. Some of these errors can go undetected by QuickBASIC until either an abnormal end occurs during execution or the program terminates with the results in error.

There are several techniques you can use for attempting to discover the portion of the program that is in error. These methods are **debugging techniques**. The errors themselves are **bugs**, and the activity involved in their detection is **debugging**. QuickBASIC has a fully integrated debugger which pinpoints errors by tracing, or highlighting, through the QuickBASIC source code. The QuickBASIC debugging features include the following:

- Examining values through the immediate window
- Executing one statement at a time
- Breakpoints
- Tracing
- Set next statement
- Recording
- Watch variables and watchpoints

EXAMINING VALUES THROUGH THE IMMEDIATE WINDOW

Following the termination of execution of a program, the program's variables remain equal to the latest values assigned. Through the immediate window, you can examine their values. This is an easy-to-use, and yet, powerful debugging tool.

To activate the immediate window, press F6. You may then display the value of any variables in the program by using the PRINT statement and the names of the variables. Recall that when a statement is entered in the immediate window, it is executed immediately. After viewing the values, press F6 to deactivate the immediate window and activate the view window.

If you have a mouse, move the pointer to the inactive window and click the mouse button.

EXECUTING ONE STATEMENT AT A TIME

Another debugging tool is the Step mode. In the **Step mode**, the PC executes the program one statement at a time. To activate this mode, press the F8 key. The first time you press the F8 key, the PC displays the first executable statement in reverse video. Thereafter, each time you press the F8 key, the PC executes the statement in reverse video and displays the next executable statement in reverse video. Hence, the PC steps through the program one statement at a time as you press the F8 key.

While the PC is in the Step mode and before you press the F8 key again, you can do any of the following to better understand what the program is doing:

- Activate the immediate window and use the PRINT statement to display the values of variables.
- Use the F4 key to toggle between displaying the program and the output screen.
- Modify any statement in the program. If you modify the statement in reverse video, the reverse video disappears. It reappears as soon as you move the cursor off the line.

To exit the Step mode, press the F5 key. The F5 key continues normal execution of the program. If you want to halt the program again, press Ctrl + Break. To continue execution after pressing Ctrl + Break, you can do one of the following:

- Press F5 to continue normal execution
- Press Shift + F5 to start execution from the beginning of the program
- Press F8 to activate the Step mode

BREAKPOINTS

A **breakpoint** is a line in the program where you want execution to halt. Breakpoints are established by moving the cursor to the line in question, followed by pressing the F9 key or selecting the Toggle Breakpoint command in the Debug menu. When you execute the program after setting one or more breakpoints, the PC halts execution at the next breakpoint and displays it in reverse video. Once the program halts at a breakpoint, you can do one of the following:

- Press the F8 key to enter the Step mode and execute from the one statement at a time to the next breakpoint
- Display the values of variables in the immediate window
- Edit the program
- Delete or add new breakpoints
- Press F5 to continue execution of the program

To toggle off a breakpoint, move the cursor to the breakpoint and press the F9 key. An alternative method for clearing breakpoints is to select the command Clear All Breakpoints in the Debug menu. This latter method can be useful, especially when you have set a number of breakpoints and cannot remember where they are located in the program. A breakpoint only displays in reverse video when it halts execution of the program.

To save time, you should carefully select breakpoints. Commonly used breakpoints include lines immediately following input, calculations, and decision statements.

TRACING

T he Trace On command in the Debug menu causes the PC to trace the program. **Tracing** means that the program will execute in slow motion. As the program executes in slow motion, the PC highlights each statement as it executes it. With the Trace On command you can quickly get an idea as to flow of control in your program. This activity must be observed to be appreciated.

The Trace On command works like a toggle switch. Select it once and the PC will trace the flow of control. Select it again, and you turn tracing off. You know that tracing is on when there is a bullet in front of the command in the Debug menu. If you are using the commercial version of QuickBASIC, note that you must toggle on Full Menus in the Option menu for the Trace On command to display in the Debug menu.

Two QuickBASIC statements that carry out the same function as the Trace On command are TRON and TROFF. The TRON statement turns on tracing for all future statements executed. The TROFF statement turns tracing off. Although most QuickBASIC programmers use the Trace On command to trace a program, some find the TRON and TROFF statements useful for tracing small sections of a program.

SET NEXT STATEMENT

T he Set Next Statement command in the Debug menu allows you to establish with the cursor where execution will continue following a program halt. For example, assume that you have set a breakpoint in a program. When the PC halts execution at the statement, you can move the cursor to any line in the program and select the Set Next Statement command. When execution resumes, it will begin at the cursor rather than at the statement in reverse video. The Set Next Statement command works much like the infamous GOTO statement. Use caution when evaluating the program results following the use of this command since skipping over code can produce unexpected results. If you are using the commercial version of QuickBASIC, note that you must toggle on Full Menus in the Option menu for the Trace On command to display in the Debug menu.

RECORDING

*T*he History On command in the Debug menu is often used in conjunction with breakpoints. When you select the History On command, the PC records the last 20 lines executed by the program. When the program halts at a breakpoint, you can use the Shift + F8 to go back through the last 20 lines executed. You can use the Shift + F10 to go forward through the last 20 lines executed.

Stepping through the last 20 lines can also be useful when your program halts due to a logic error. If you select History On prior to execution, then you can step through the last 20 lines executed before the program's premature termination.

To stop recording the last 20 lines, select History On. This command acts like a toggle switch. Select it once and it's on. Select it again and it's off. You know that the History On command is active when there is a bullet in front of the command in the Debug menu. (Full Menus in the Option menu must be active for the History On command to display in the Debug menu.)

WATCH VARIABLES AND WATCHPOINTS

*T*he Add Watch command in the Debug menu allows you to enter the names of variables or expressions that you want displayed in the watch window. The **watch window** (Figure A-1) displays above the view window whenever watch variables are active. Watching a variable is often combined with the Step mode (F8) or breakpoints to track its value, thus avoiding repeated use of the PRINT statement in the immediate window.

FIGURE A-1
The watch window displays above the view window. Program halts on LOOP statement when Emp.Number$ = "128". Value of Emp.Hours is 38. Value of Emp.Rate is 4.6.

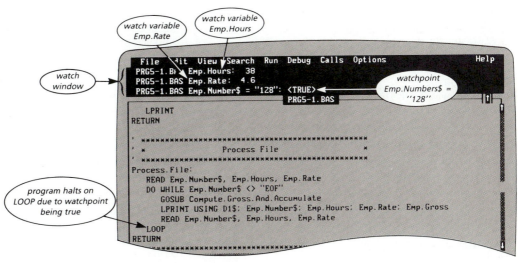

With the commercial version of QuickBASIC, you can add watch variables or conditions to the watch window by pressing Shift + F9 or selecting the Instant Watch command. The main difference between the Instant Watch and Add Watch commands is that with Instant Watch you do not have to type the variable name or condition. You simply select a watch variable by moving the cursor within the variable name in the program. To select a condition, you must use the Shift and arrow keys to highlight it before pressing Shift + F9.

The Watchpoint command in the Debug menu allows you to enter a watchpoint in the watch window. A **watchpoint** (Figure A-1) is a condition that halts program execution when it becomes true.

To delete individual watch variables or watchpoints, select the Delete Watch command in the Debug menu. To delete all watch variables and watch points, select the Delete All Watch command.

QuickBASIC Index

MICROSOFT QuickBASIC REFERENCE CARD

Legend: Uppercase letters are required keywords. You must supply items within < >'s. You must select one of the entries within { }'s. Items within [ ]'s are optional. Three ellipsis points (...) indicate that an item may be repeated as many times as you wish. The symbol **b** represents a blank character.

Summary of BASIC Statements

STATEMENT

BEEP
Causes the speaker on the PC to beep for a fraction of a second.

CALL <name> [(argumentlist)]
Transfers control to a subprogram.

CHAIN <"filespec">
Instructs the PC to stop executing the current program, load another program from auxiliary storage and start executing it.

CHDIR <pathspecification>
Changes the current directory for the specified drive.

CIRCLE <(x, y), radius> [,color [,start,end [,shape]]]
Causes the PC to draw an ellipse, circle, arc, or wedge with center at (x, y).

CLEAR [,,stack]
Reinitializes all program variables, closes files, and sets the stack size.

CLOSE [#] [filenumber] [,[#] [filenumber]]...
Closes specified files.

CLS
Erases the information on the screen and places the cursor in the upper left corner of the screen.

COLOR [background] [,palette]
COLOR [foreground] [,background] [,border]
In the text mode, defines the color of the foreground characters, background, and border around the screen.

COM(n) {**ON** / **OFF** / **STOP**} Enables or disables trapping of communications activity on adaptor n.

COMMON [SHARED] <variable> [,variable]...
Passes specified variables to a chained program.

CONST <constantname> = <expression> [, constantname = expression]...
Declares symbolic constants that can be used in place of numeric or string expressions.

STATEMENT

DATA <data item> [,data item]...
Provides for the creation of a sequence of data items for use by the READ statement.

DATE$ = mm {**/** / **-**} **dd** {**/** / **-**} **yy[yy]** Sets the system date, where mm = month, dd = day, yy = year, yyyy = 4-digit year.

DECLARE {**FUNCTION** / **SUB**} **name [(parameterlist)]**
Declares references to QuickBASIC procedures and invokes argument-type checking.

DEF FN<name> [(variable, [, variable]...)] = <expression>
Defines and names a function that can be referenced in a program as often as needed. Multiline functions end with an END DEF statement.

DEFtype <letterrange> [,letterrange]...
Sets the data type for variables and functions.

DIM [SHARED] <arrayname(size)> [AS type],
[arrayname(size) [AS type]]...
Reserves storage locations for arrays and declares the array type.

DO
Causes the statements between DO and LOOP to be executed repeatedly. The loop is controlled by a condition in the corresponding LOOP statement.

DO UNTIL <condition>
Causes the statements between DO UNTIL and LOOP to be executed repeatedly until the condition is true.

DO WHILE <condition>
Causes the statements between DO WHILE and LOOP to be executed repeatedly while the condition is true.

DRAW <string expression>
Causes the PC to draw the object that is defined by the value of the string expression.

END {**DEF** / **FUNCTION** / **IF** / **SELECT** / **SUB** / **TYPE**} Ends a QuickBASIC program, procedure, or block of code.

ERASE <arrayname> [,arrayname]...
Eliminates previously defined arrays.

ERROR <integerexpression>
Simulates the occurrence of a QuickBASIC error or allows the user to define error codes.

EXIT <statement>
Exits statement, where statement is equal to FOR, DO, DEF, FUNCTION, or SUB.

STATEMENT

FIELD <#filenumber, width AS string variable>
[, width AS string variable]...
Allocates space for variables in a random file buffer.

FILES [filespecification]
Lists the names of all programs and data files in auxiliary storage on the default drive or the drive specified by file specification.

FOR <loopvariable> = <initial> TO <limit>
[STEP increment]
Causes the statements between the FOR and NEXT statements to be executed until the value of loopvariable exceeds the value of the limit.

FUNCTION <name> [(parameterlist)] [STATIC]
Declares the name, the parameters, and initiates a function procedure that ends with an END FUNCTION.

GET <(x₁, y₁) - (x₂, y₂), arrayname>
Reads the colors of the points in the specified area on the screen into an array.

GET <[#][filenumber] [,record number]
Reads the specified record from a random file and transfers it to the buffer that is defined by the corresponding FIELD statement.

GOSUB {**linelabel** / **linenumber**} Causes control to transfer to a subroutine beginning at the specified line. Also retains the location of the next statement following the GOSUB statement.

GOTO {**linelabel** / **linenumber**} Transfers control to the specified line.

IF <condition> THEN [clause] [ELSE [clause]]
The single line IF statement causes execution of the THEN clause if the condition is true. If the ELSE clause is included, it causes execution of the ELSE clause if the condition is false.

IF <condition> THEN
[statementblock₁]
[ELSE
[statementblock₂]]
END IF
The block IF statement allows for multiple lines in the THEN and ELSE clauses. Causes execution of the THEN clause if the condition is true. Causes execution of the ELSE clause if the condition is false. The ELSE IF <condition> THEN clause may be used in place of the ELSE clause.

INPUT [;][,"prompt message" {**;** / **,**}**] <variable> [,variable]...**
Provides for the assignment of values to variables from a source external to the program, such as the keyboard.

INPUT <#filenumber, variable> [,variable]...
Provides for the assignment of values to variables from a sequential file in auxiliary storage.

(*BASIC Statements* continued on page R.2 in left column)

MICROSOFT QuickBASIC REFERENCE CARD

Summary of BASIC Statements (continued)

STATEMENT

KEY {n, string value / ON / OFF / LIST}
Assigns a string value to a function key. Also used to display the values and enable or disable the function key display line.

KEY(n) {ON / OFF / STOP}
Activates or deactivates trapping of the specified key n.

KILL <filespecification>
Deletes a file from disk.

[LET] <variable> = <expression>
Causes the evaluation of the expression, followed by the assignment of the resulting value to the variable to the left of the equal sign.

LINE [(x₁, y₁)] - (x₂, y₂)> [,color] [,B[F]][,Style]
Draws a line or a box on the screen.

LINE INPUT [;]["prompt message";] <string variable> or
LINE INPUT <#filenumber,> <string variable>
Provides for the assignment of a line up to 255 characters from a source external to the program, such as the keyboard or a sequential file.

LOCATE [row] [,column] [,cursor] [,start] [,stop]
Positions the cursor on the screen. Can also be used to make the cursor visible or invisible and to control the size of the cursor.

LOCK <[#]filenumber>,` [,record / [start] TO end]
Locks all or some of the records in a file.

LOOP {WHILE / UNTIL b} [condition] Identifies the end of a loop.

LPRINT [item] [{,/;} item]... Provides for the generation of output to the printer.

LPRINT USING <string expression> <item> [{,/;/b} item]...
Provides for the generation of formatted output to the printer.

LSET <string variable> = <string expression>
Moves string data left-justified into an area of a random file buffer that is defined by the string variable.

MID$ <(string var, start position [,number]> = <substring>
Replaces a substring within a string.

MKDIR <pathname>
Creates a new directory.

NAME <oldfilespecification> AS <newfilespecification>
Renames a file on disk.

STATEMENT

NEXT [numeric variable] [,numeric variable]...
Identifies the end of the For loop(s).

ON COM(n) GOSUB {linelabel / linenumber}
Causes control to transfer to the specified line when data is filling the communications buffer (n).

ON ERROR GOTO {linelabel / linenumber}
Enables error trapping and specifies the first line of an error-handling routine that the PC is to branch to in the event of an error. If linenumber is zero, error trapping is disabled.

ON <numeric expression> **GOSUB** {linelabel-list / linenumber-list}
Causes control to transfer to the subroutine represented by the selected line. Also retains the location of the next statement following the ON-GOSUB statement.

ON <numeric expression> **GOTO** {linelabel-list / linenumber-list}
Causes control to transfer to one of several lines according to the value of the numeric expression.

ON KEY(n) GOSUB {linelabel / linenumber}
Causes control to transfer to the specified line when the function key or cursor control key (n) is pressed.

ON PEN GOSUB {linelabel / linenumber}
Causes control to transfer to the specified line when the light pen is activated.

ON PLAY(n) GOSUB {linelabel / linenumber}
Plays continuous background music. Transfers control to the specified line when a note (n) is sensed.

ON STRIG(n) GOSUB {linelabel / linenumber}
Causes control to transfer to the specified line when one of the joystick buttons (n) is pressed.

ON TIMER(n) GOSUB {linelabel / linenumber}
Causes control to transfer to the specified line when the specified period of time (n) in seconds has elapsed.

ON UEVENT GOSUB {linelabel / linenumber}
Defines the event-handler for a user-defined event.

OPEN <filespec> **FOR** <mode> **AS** <[#]filenumber> [LEN = record length]
Allows a program to read or write records to a file. If record length is specified, then the file is opened as a random file. If the record length is not specified, then the file is opened as a sequential file.

STATEMENT

OPTION BASE {0 / 1}
Assigns a lower bound of 0 or 1 to all arrays declared with only an upper-bound value.

OUT <port>, <data>
Sends a byte to a machine I/O port.

PAINT <(x, y)> [(,paint] [,boundary]]
Paints an area on the screen with the selected color.

PALETTE [attribute, color] or
PALETTE USING <arrayname> [(arrayindex)]
Changes one or more of the colors in the palette.

PCOPY <sourcepage>, <destinationpage>
Copies one screen page to another.

PEN(n) {ON / OFF / STOP}
Enables or disables the PEN read function used to analyze light pen activity.

PLAY <string expression>
Causes the PC to play music according to the value of the string expression.

PLAY {ON / OFF / STOP}
Enables, disables, or suspends play event trapping.

POKE <address>, <byte>
Writes a byte into a storage location.

PRESET <(x, y)> [,color]
Draws a point in the color specified at (x, y). If no color is specified, it erases the point.

PRINT [item] [{,/;} item]... Provides for the generation of output to the screen.

PRINT <#filenumber,> [item] [{,/;/b} item]...
Provides for the generation of output to a sequential file.

PRINT USING <string expression;> <item> [{,/;} item]...
Provides for the generation of formatted output to the screen.

PRINT <#filenumber,> **USING** <string expression;>
<item> [{,/;/b} item]...
Provides for the generation of formatted output to a sequential file.

(BASIC Statements continued on page R.3 in left column)

MICROSOFT QuickBASIC REFERENCE CARD

Summary of BASIC Statements (continued)

STATEMENT

PSET <(x, y)> [,color]
Draws a point in the color specified at (x, y).

PUT <(x_1, y_1), arrayname> [,action]
Writes the colors of the points in the array onto an area of the screen.

PUT <[#]filenumber> [,record number]
Writes a record to a random file from a buffer defined by the corresponding FIELD statement.

RANDOMIZE [numeric expression]
Reseeds the random number generator.

READ <variable> [,variable]...
Provides for the assignment of values to variables from a sequence of data items created from DATA statements.

REDIM [SHARED] <arrayname(size)> [AS type]...
Changes the space allocated to an array declared $DYNAMIC.

{REM / '} {comment}
Provides for the insertion of comments in a program.

RESET
Closes all disk files.

RESTORE {linelabel / linenumber}
Allows the data items in DATA statements to be reread.

RESUME {linelabel / NEXT / 0 / b / linenumber}
Continues program execution at the linelabel, or the line following that which caused the error, after an error-recovery procedure.

RETURN {linelabel / linenumber}
Causes control to transfer from a subroutine back to the statement that follows the corresponding GOSUB or ON-GOSUB statement.

RMDIR <pathname>
Removes a directory from disk after all files and subdirectories have been removed.

RSET <string variable> = <string expression>
Moves string data right-justified into an area of a random file buffer that is defined by string variable.

RUN {linenumber / linelabel / b}
Restarts the program in main storage.

SCREEN [mode] [,color switch] [,active page] [,visual page]
Sets the screen attributes for text mode, medium-resolution graphics, or high-resolution graphics.

SEEK <[#]filenumber> , <position>
Sets the position in a file for the next read or write.

STATEMENT

SELECT CASE <testexpression>
CASE <$matchexpression_1$>
    [range of statements₁]
[CASE <$matchexpression_2$>
    [range of statements₂]
    .
    .
[CASE ELSE
    [range of statements₂]
END SELECT
Causes execution of one of several ranges of statements depending on the value of testexpression.

SHARED <variable> [AS type] [,variable [AS type]]...
Gives a SUB or FUNCTION procedure access to variables declared at the module level without passing them as parameters.

SHELL [commandstring]
Places the current QB session in a temporary wait state and returns control to MS-DOS. Can also execute another program or MS-DOS command as specified in commandstring.

SLEEP [seconds]
Suspends execution of the calling program.

SOUND <frequency>, <duration>
Causes the generation of sound through the PC speaker.

STATIC <variablelist>
Causes variables and arrays to be local to either a DEF FN, a FUNCTION, or a SUB, and maintains values between calls.

STOP
Stops execution of a program. Unlike the END statement, files are left open.

STRIG(n) {ON / OFF / STOP}
Enables or disables trapping of the joystick buttons.

SUB <globalname> [(parameterlist)] [STATIC]
Establishes the beginning of a subprogram. The end of the subprogram is identified by the END SUB statement.

SWAP <$variable_1$>, <$variable_2$>
Exchanges the values of two variables or two elements of an array.

SYSTEM
Closes all open files and returns control to MS-DOS.

TIME$ = hh[:mm[:ss]]
Sets the system time, where hh = hours, mm = minutes, and ss = seconds.

TIMER {ON / OFF / STOP}
Enables or disables trapping of timed events.

STATEMENT

TROFF
Disables statement tracing.

TRON
Causes the PC to trace execution of program statements.

TYPE <labelname>
    <$fieldname_1$> AS <fieldtype>
    .
    .
    <$fieldname_n$,> AS <fieldtype>
END TYPE
Creates user-defined data types containing one or more elements.

UEVENT {ON / OFF / STOP}
Enables, disables, or suspends user-defined event trapping.

UNLOCK <[#]filenumber> , {record / [start] TO end}
Unlocks records in a file.

VIEW [[SCREEN] (x_1, y_1) – (x_2, y_2)] [,color] [,boundary]
Defines a viewport.

VIEW PRINT [topline TO bottomline]
Establishes boundaries for the screen text viewport.

WEND
Identifies the end of a While loop.

WHILE <condition>
Identifies the beginning of a While loop. Causes the statements between WHILE and WEND to be executed repeatedly while the condition is true.

WIDTH {40 / 80}
Erases the information on the screen, sets the width of the line on the screen to 40 or 80 characters, and places the cursor in the upper left corner of the screen.

WIDTH LPRINT <width>
Sets the printer column width.

WINDOW <[SCREEN] (x_1, y_1) – (x_2, y_2)>
Redefines the coordinates of the viewport. Allows you to draw objects in space and not be bounded by the limits of the screen.

WRITE [expression list]
Writes data to the screen.

WRITE <[#]filenumber,> [item] {; / ,} [item]...
Writes data to a sequential file. Causes the PC to insert commas between the items written to the sequential file.

MICROSOFT QuickBASIC REFERENCE CARD

Summary of BASIC Functions

FUNCTION

ABS(N)
Returns the absolute value of the argument N.

ASC(X$)
Returns a two-digit numeric value that is equivalent in ASCII code to the first character of the string argument X$.

ATN(N)
Returns the angle in radians whose tangent is the value of the argument N.

CDBL(N)
Returns N converted to a double-precision value.

CHR$(N)
Returns a single string character that is equivalent in ASCII code to the numeric argument N.

CINT(N)
Returns N converted to an integer after rounding the fractional part of N.

CLNG(N)
Returns N converted to a long integer after rounding the fractional part of N.

COMMAND$
Returns the command line used to start the program.

COS(N)
Returns the cosine of the argument N where N is in radians.

CSNG(N)
Returns N converted to a single-precision value.

CSRLIN
Returns the vertical (row) coordinate of the cursor.

CVI(X$), CVL(X$), CVS(X$), CVD(X$)
Returns the integer, long integer, single-precision, or double-precision numeric value equivalent to the string X$. Used with random files.

DATE$
Returns the current date (mm-dd-yyyy).

EOF(filenumber)
Returns −1 (true) if the end-of-file has been sensed on the sequential file associated with filenumber. Returns 0 (false) if the end-of-file has not been sensed.

ERDEV
Returns an error code from the last device that caused an error.

FUNCTION

ERDEV$
Returns a string expression containing the name of the device that generated a vital error.

ERL
Returns the line number preceding the line that caused the error. If no line numbers are used, then ERL returns a zero.

ERR
Returns the error code for the last error that occurred.

EXP(N)
Returns e(2.718281....) raised to the argument N.

FILEATTR
Returns the file mode for an open file.

FIX(N)
Returns the value of N truncated to an integer.

FRE(N)
Returns the amount of available stack space (N = −2), string space (N not equal to −1 or −2), or size in bytes of the largest array you can create (N = −1).

FREEFILE
Returns the next free QuickBASIC file number.

HEX$(N)
Returns the hexadecimal equivalent of N.

INKEY$
Returns the last character entered from the keyboard.

INP(N)
Returns the byte read from an I/O port N.

INPUT$(N)
Suspends execution of the program until a string of N characters is received from the keyboard.

INPUT$(N, [#]filenumber)
Returns a string of characters from the specified file.

INSTR(P, X$, S$)
Returns the beginning position of the substring S$ in string X$. P indicates the position at which the search begins in the string X$.

INT(N)
Returns the largest integer that is less than or equal to the argument N.

LBOUND(arrayname[,dimension])
Returns the lower-bound value for the specified dimension of arrayname.

FUNCTION

LCASE$(X$)
Returns X$ in all lowercase letters.

LEFT$(X$, N)
Returns the leftmost N characters of the string argument X$.

LEN(X$)
Returns the length of the string argument X$.

LOC(#filenumber)
With a random file, it returns the number of the last record read or written. With a sequential file, it returns the number of records read from or written to the file.

LOF(#filenumber)
Returns the number of bytes allocated to a file.

LOG(N)
Returns the natural log of the argument N where N is greater than 0.

LPOS(N)
Returns the current position of the line printer's print head within the printer buffer where N is equal to 1 for LPT1, 2 for LPT2, and so on.

LTRIM$(X$)
Returns X$ with leading spaces removed.

MID$(X$, P, N)
Returns N characters of the string argument X$ beginning at position P.

MKI$(N), MKL$(N), MKS$(N), MKD$(N)
Returns the string equivalent of an integer, long integer, single-precision, or double-precision value. Used with random files.

OCT$(N)
Returns the octal equivalent of N.

PEEK(N)
Returns the value of the byte stored at the specified storage location N.

PEN(N)
Returns light pen coordinate information. The information is dependent on the value assigned to N.

PLAY(n)
Returns the number of notes currently in the music background buffer.

PMAP (c, n)
Returns the world coordinate of the physical coordinate c or vice versa. The parameter n varies between 0 and 3, and determines whether c is an x or y coordinate, and whether the coordinate is to be mapped from the physical to the world coordinate or vice versa.

(BASIC Functions continued on page R.5 in left column)

MICROSOFT QuickBASIC REFERENCE CARD

Summary of BASIC Functions (continued)

FUNCTION

POINT { (x, y) }
    { (n) }
With the argument (x, y), the PC returns the foreground color attribute of the point (x, y). With the argument n, the PC returns the physical or world x or y coordinate of the last point referenced. The parameter n varies in the range 0 to 3.

POS(0)
Returns the current position of the cursor on the screen.

RIGHT$(X$, N)
Returns the rightmost N characters of the string argument X$.

RND(N)
Returns a random number between 0 (inclusive) and 1 (exclusive). If N is positive or not included, the next random number is returned. If N is 0 (zero), the previous random number is returned. If N is negative, the random number generator is reseeded before a random number is returned.

RTRIM$(X$)
Returns X$ with trailing spaces removed.

SCREEN(row, column)
Returns the ASCII code for the character at the specified row (line) and column on the screen.

SEEK(filenumber)
Returns the current file position.

SGN(N)
Returns the sign of the argument N: −1 if the argument N is less than 0; 0 if the argument N is equal to 0; or +1 if the argument N is greater than 0.

SIN(N)
Returns the sine of the argument N where N is in radians.

SPACE$(N)
Returns a string of N spaces.

SPC(N)
Displays N spaces. Can be used only in an output statement such as PRINT or LPRINT.

SQR(N)
Returns the square root of the positive argument N.

STICK(N)
Returns the x and y coordinates of joystick N.

STR$(N)
Returns the string equivalent of the numeric argument N.

STRIG(n)
Returns the status of the joystick buttons.

STRING$(N, X$)
Returns N times the first character of X$.

FUNCTION

TAB(N)
Causes the PC to tab over to position N on the output device. Can be used only in an output statement such as PRINT or LPRINT.

TAN(N)
Returns the tangent of the argument N where N is in radians.

TIMER
Returns a value that is equal to the number of seconds elapsed since midnight.

TIME$
Returns the current time (hh:mm:ss).

UBOUND(arrayname[,dimension])
Returns the upper-bound value for the specified dimension of arrayname.

UCASE$(X$)
Returns X$ in all uppercase letters.

VAL(X$)
Returns the numeric equivalent of the string argument X$.

VARPTR(variablename)
Returns the storage address of variablename.

VARPTR$(variablename)
Returns a string representation of the storage address of variablename for use in DRAW and PLAY statements.

Summary of All Operators

ORDER OF PRECEDENCE	OPERATOR	SYMBOL
Highest	Arithmetic	^
		* or /
		+ or − [Unary + or − sign]
		MOD
		+ or − [Binary + or − sign]
	Concatenation	+
	Relational	=, >, > =, <, < =, or <>
	Logical	NOT
		AND
		OR or XOR
		EQV
Lowest		IMP

Summary of Command Line Options

For the desired effect, append one or more of the following to the QB or QBI command when you enter QuickBASIC:

OPTION	FUNCTION
/ah	Permits arrays to exceed 64 KB.
/b	Designates monochrome display.
/c:size	Sets the size of the communications port buffer.
/cmd str	Passes the string str to the COMMAND$ function.
file	Loads and displays the QuickBASIC program file
/g	Designates faster video output.
/h	Designates maximum resolution for the video device.
/l [lib]	Loads the specified library or QB.QLB if lib is omitted
/mbf	Causes conversion functions to treat IEEE-format numbers as Microsoft binary format numbers.
/nohi	Allows monitor that does not support high intensity.
/run file	Loads and executes the QuickBASIC program file before displaying it.

Limits to QuickBASIC

	MAXIMUM	MINIMUM
Variable name	40 characters	1 character
String length	32,767 characters	0 characters
Array dimensions	60	1
Array subscript value	32,767	−32,768
Integers	32,767	−32,768
Long integers	2,147,483,647	−2,147,483,648
Single precision (+)	3.402823E + 38	1.401298E−45
Single precision (−)	−1.401298E−45	−3.402823E + 38
Double precision (+)	1.797693134862315D + 308	4.940656458412465D−324
Double precision (−)	−4.940656458412465D−324	−1.797693134862315D + 308

Variable Type Definition

APPEND CHARACTER	DECLARATION
%	Integer variable
&	Long integer variable
!	Single-precision variable
#	Double-precision variable
$	String variable

MICROSOFT QuickBASIC REFERENCE CARD

Cursor Movement Keys

KEYS	FUNCTION
←	Character left
→	Character right
↓	Down one line
↑	Up one line
Ctrl + ←	Word left
Ctrl + →	Word right
Ctrl + End	End of program
Ctrl + Enter	Beginning of next line
Ctrl + Home	Beginning of program
Ctrl + Q + E	Top of window
Ctrl + Q + S	Beginning of current line
Ctrl + Q + X	Bottom of window
End	End of line
Home	First indent of current line
Tab	Tab to next tab setting

Scroll Keys

KEYS	FUNCTION
Ctrl + ↓	Line down
Ctrl + ↑	Line up
Page Down	Page down
Page Up	Page up
Ctrl + Page Down	Left one full screen
Ctrl + Page Up	Right one full screen

Execution and Debugging Keys

KEYS	FUNCTION
F5	Continues execution from current statement.
Shift + F5	Starts execution from beginning.
F7	Executes program to cursor.
F8	Executes next program statement.
Shift + F8	Traces execution history backward.
F9	Toggles the Debug menu Breakpoint command.
Shift + F9	Instant watch.
F10	Single step, tracing around a procedure call.
Shift + F10	Traces execution history forward.

Search Keys

KEYS	FUNCTION
F3	Repeats the last find.
Ctrl + \	Searches for selected (highlighted) text.

Help Keys

KEYS	FUNCTION
F1	Displays help on the item in which the cursor is located.
Shift + F1	Displays help on help.
Alt + F1	Displays previously requested help topic. (Repeat up to 20 times.)
Ctrl + F1	Displays next help topic in Help file.
Shift + Ctrl + F1	Displays previous help topic in Help file.
Alt + H	Displays help through Help menu commands.
Esc	Clears help from the screen.
Letter	Moves cursor to help-topic title beginning with letter entered.
Shift + letter	Moves cursor to previous help-topic title beginning with letter entered.
Tab	Moves cursor to next help-topic title in help screen.
Shift + Tab	Moves cursor to previous help-topic title in help screen.

Insert and Copy Keys

KEYS	FUNCTION
Insert	Toggles insert or overtype.
Ctrl + Insert	Copies selection to clipboard and keeps.
Shift + Insert	Inserts contents of clipboard.
Shift + Delete	Copies selection to clipboard and deletes.
Ctrl + Y	Copies current line to clipboard and deletes.
Ctrl + Q + Y	Copies from cursor to end of line to clipboard and deletes.

Delete Keys

KEYS	FUNCTION
Backspace	Deletes character to left.
Ctrl + T	Deletes rest of word.
Delete	Deletes character at cursor or selected text.
Shift + Tab	Deletes leading spaces from selected lines.

Selection (Highlight) Keys

KEYS	FUNCTION
Shift + ←	Character left
Shift + →	Character right
Shift + Ctrl + →	Word right
Shift + Ctrl + ←	Word left
Shift + ↓	Current line
Shift + ↑	Line above
Shift + Page Down	Screen down
Shift + Page Up	Screen up
Shift + Ctrl + Home	To beginning of program
Shift + Ctrl + End	To end of program

View Keys

KEYS	FUNCTION
F4	Toggles between view window and output screen.
F6	Makes next window the active one.

Reserved Words

ABS	ELSEIF	LOOP	SCREEN
ACCESS	END	LPOS	SEEK
ALIAS	ENDIF	LPRINT	SEG
AND	ENVIRON	LSET	SELECT
ANY	ENVIRON$	LTRIM$	SETMEM
APPEND	EOF	MID$	SGN
AS	EQV	MKD$	SHARED
ASC	ERASE	MKDIR	SHELL
ATN	ERDEV	MKDMBF$	SIGNAL
BASE	ERDEV$	MKI$	SIN
BEEP	ERL	MKS$	SINGLE
BINARY	ERR	MKSMBF$	SLEEP
BLOAD	ERROR	MOD	SOUND
BSAVE	EXIT	NAME	SPACE$
CALL	EXP	NEXT	SPC
CALLS	FIELD	NOT	SQR
CASE	FILEATTR	OCT$	STATIC
CDBL	FILES	OFF	STEP
CDECL	FIX	ON	STICK
CHAIN	FOR	OPEN	STOP
CHDIR	FRE	OPTION	STR$
CHR$	FREEFILE	OR	STRIG
CINT	FUNCTION	OUT	STRING
CIRCLE	GET	OUTPUT	STRING$
CLEAR	GOSUB	PAINT	SUB
CLOSE	GOTO	PALETTE	SWAP
CLS	HEX$	PCOPY	SYSTEM
COLOR	IF	PEEK	TAB
COM	IMP	PEN	TAN
COMMAND$	INKEY$	PLAY	THEN
COMMON	INP	PMAP	TIME$
CONST	INPUT	POINT	TIMER
COS	INPUT$	POKE	TO
CSNG	INSTR	POS	TROFF
CSRLIN	INT	PRESET	TRON
CVD	INTEGER	PRINT	TYPE
CVDMBF	IOCTL	PRINT#	UBOUND
CVI	IOCTL$	PSET	UCASE$
CVL	IS	PUT	UNLOCK
CVS	KEY	RANDOM	UNTIL
CVSMBF	KILL	RANDOMIZE	USING
DATA	LBOUND	READ	VAL
DATE$	LCASE$	REDIM	VARPTR
DECLARE	LEFT$	REM	VARPTR$
DEF	LEN	RESET	VARSEG
DEFDBL	LET	RESTORE	VIEW
DEFINT	LINE	RESUME	WAIT
DEFLNG	LIST	RETURN	WEND
DEFSNG	LOC	RIGHT$	WHILE
DEFSTR	LOCAL	RMDIR	WIDTH
DIM	LOCATE	RND	WINDOW
DO	LOCK	RSET	WRITE
DOUBLE	LOF	RUN	WRITE#
DRAW	LOG	SADD	XOR
ELSE	LONG		